ROME AND CONSTANTINOPLE

SAINTS PETER AND ANDREW LECTURES

ROME AND CONSTANTINOPLE

Essays in the Dialogue of Love

Edited by
Robert Barringer

Holy Cross Orthodox Press
Brookline, Massachusetts 02146
1984

© Copyright 1984 by Holy Cross Orthodox Press

All rights reserved.

Published by Holy Cross Orthodox Press
50 Goddard Avenue
Brookline, Massachusetts 02146

Cover design by Mary C. Vaporis

Library of Congress Cataloging in Publication Data
   Main entry under title:

   Rome and Constantinople: essays in the dialogue of love.

   (Saints Peter and Andrew lectures)
   Bibliography: p.
   Contents: Rome and Byzantium/ Michael A. Fahey—The experience of God in the Orthodox tradition/ Daniel J. Sahas—Catholic-Orthodox dialogue/ Robert Barringer—[etc.]
      1. Orthodox Eastern Church—Relations—Catholic Church—Addresses, essays, lectures. 2. Catholic Church—Relations—Orthodox Eastern Church—Addresses, essays, lectures. 3. Feminism—Religious aspects—Orthodox Eastern Church—Addresses, essays, lectures. 4. Orthodox Eastern Church—Doctrines—Addresses, essays, lectures. I. Barringer, Robert. II. Series.
   BX324.3.R66   281.9   84-25139
   ISBN 0-917651—04—9 (pbk.)

CONTENTS

FOREWORD
Robert Barringer C.S.B.   7

ROME AND BYZANTIUM: SISTER CHURCHES PREPARE FOR THE THIRD MILLENNIUM
Michael A. Fahey S.J.   9

THE EXPERIENCE OF GOD IN THE ORTHODOX TRADITION
Daniel J. Sahas   35

CATHOLIC—ORTHODOX DIALOGUE: THE PRESENT POSITION
Robert Barringer C.S.B.   55

FEMINIST THEOLOGY: AN ORTHODOX CHRISTIAN PERSPECTIVE
Deborah Belonick   73

NOTES ON THE CONTRIBUTORS   86

Foreword

The St. Peter and St. Andrew Lectures were begun at the University of St. Michael's College as a private initiative that might provide occasions for a much neglected dialogue—practical as well as theological—between Roman Catholic and Orthodox Christians in Toronto. It was hoped that the two groups might begin to speak to one another frankly and helpfully about the things deepest to their own experience as Christians, and as Christians formed by traditions that have been estranged from one another for much too long. The Inaugural Lecture on February 22, 1982 was attended by His Eminence, Emmett Cardinal Carter, Archbishop of Toronto and by His Grace, Soterios, Bishop of the Greek Orthodox Diocese of Toronto (Canada), and the Lectures have continued to enjoy the support and encouragement of both hierarchs ever since.

The true patrons of this initiative, however, are the two brothers, Peter and Andrew, who were chosen by Christ as his apostles and sent out into the world to work side by side, not as the fishermen they once were, but as fishers of men: ἁλιεῖς ἀνθρώπων. The two brothers are now the patrons of the Church of Rome and the Church of Constantinople; they were and still are extraordinary figures, powerful to intercede on behalf of our prayers, if we truly desire the unity of the Body of Christ. Following the example of recent popes and ecumenical patriarchs, the format of the series calls for a Roman Catholic theologian to speak in February on or around the time of the feast of the Chair of Saint Peter (February 22) and for an Orthodox theologian to speak in November, on or around the feast of Saint Andrew (November 30).

The initiative is one of hope and the difficulties that still bar the road towards full communion between Orthodox and Roman Catholics are not to be treated lightly. But one thing only is certain. No international dialogue of theologians and professional ecumenicists, no signed agreements at the highest theological and ecclesiastical levels will, of themselves, overcome the estrangement that still clouds the hearts of Catholics and Orthodox. What has always been missing until now is the desire among ordinary Catholics and ordinary Orthodox—not their leaders—to go beyond the familiar fears and resentments and caricatures, to emerge from their private solitudes in order to receive from one another's hands the gift of a deeper and richer and more complete Christian identity. Perhaps this will be the age when such a desire can awaken among ordinary believers. Certainly the abiding lesson to be learned from the Council of Florence and its aftermath is that the union of Eastern and Western Christians can never be achieved "from the top down."

The various views and judgments expressed in the Lectures are of course those of the lecturers themselves for which they alone are responsible. The editor is grateful for the cooperation he has received from all the lecturers and regrets only that many of their further remarks in the question period that followed each lecture could not be added to this record. The editor wishes, finally, to thank Dr. Daniel J. Sahas for his encouragement and vision in bringing this task to completion, and Fr. John M. Kelly C.S.B. of the University of St. Michael's College who made it possible to begin.

Robert Barringer C.S.B.

Rome and Byzantium: Sister Churches Prepare for the Third Millennium

MICHAEL A. FAHEY S. J.

On this day (February 22) which in the liturgical calendar of the Church of Rome commemorates the Chair of Saint Peter, I am especially honored to be able to share with you some theological reflections on a subject close to my heart: the future of the Eastern Orthodox and Roman Catholic dialogue of love.

On May 28, 1980, a special ship embarked from the port of Athens for the tiny Aegean island of Patmos where, according to legend, Saint John is purported to have received the revelations that comprise the Apocalypse. Among the distinguished passengers on board were some sixty Eastern Orthodox and Roman Catholic delegates, metropolitans, cardinals, bishops, and lay theologians who were to inaugurate on the following day on Patmos and then on neighboring Rhodes the first official theological consultation between these two churches to be held for centuries. For the first time since the Council of Florence in the fifteenth century, after estrangement, psychological isolation, and long-standing suspicions, members of various Eastern Orthodox churches and Roman Catholics from different parts of the world formally and officially were coming together to reflect in prayer and in study about the possiblity of re-establishing full communion between the sister churches.

Announcement of the opening date for the Patmos/Rhodes meeting had come with little advance notice. In October 1979, after returning to Rome from the United States, Pope John Paul II surprised many by making a visit to Constantinople, ancient Byzantium, modern Istanbul, where he conferred with one of the principal leaders of Eastern Orthodoxy, Ecumenical Patriarch Demetrios. Toward the end of the visit after the celebration of the Divine Liturgy, and after formal statements, the leaders of these two churches that have descended from Rome and Byzantium jointly announced that an official consultation would begin very soon in late May and early June of 1980.

That meeting in Istanbul between a Polish pope and a Turkish citizen, the Greek Orthodox Patriarch, was part of an ongoing exchange of visits and dialogue that began during and after Vatican II. Both their predecessors, Pope Paul VI and Ecumenical Patriarch Athenagoras, had initiated a series of reconciliatory meetings starting in Jerusalem in January 1964, where they first embraced in a touching amplexus of forgiveness and expectation. In the following year, 1965, delegations from Rome and from Constantinople formally stated in a mutual declaration that they wished to obliterate from memory the ancient anathemas of 1054 leveled against an ancient patriarch and pope. Since that formal lifting of the anathemas, visits had taken place each year to Rome and Constantinople, either by pope and patriarch or by their delegates, for the feast of Saint Peter in June and on November 30, the feast of Saint Andrew, a patron of Orthodoxy.

The personal commitment of the late Pope Paul VI toward effecting reunion of East and West has not received from biographers the attention it deserves. His dedication to that goal was strikingly symbolized on December 14, 1975, when in the Vatican's Sistine Chapel the personal representative of the Ecumenical Patriarch, Metropolitan Meliton, announced to Paul VI that the Pan-Orthodox Synod had authorized establishment of an inter-Orthodox theological commission to prepare for "official" dialogue with Catholics. On that occasion Pope Paul VI flabbergasted his associates and guests by greeting this news of a forthcoming commission with the dramatic gesture of falling to his knees and kissing Meliton's feet, thus evoking Saint Paul's words in Romans 10.15, citing the prophet Isaiah, "How beautiful are the feet of those who bring the good news!"

Such a dialogue of love helped create a mood by which the Patmos/Rhodes meeting became possible.[1] Since 1980, three subcommittees of the Orthodox and Roman Catholic official dialogue have been at work preparing texts on the sacramental life of our church. We await the publication of these texts with impatience.

Meanwhile to mark the sixteenth centenary of the Second Ecumenical Synod, Constantinople I, and the one thousand and fiftieth anniversary of Ephesos, several celebrations were held including one on Pentecost,

---

[1]For an overview of recent ecumenical developments throughout Orthodoxy, consult Michael A. Fahey, "Orthodox Ecumenicism and Theology: 1970-1978," *Theological Studies* 39 (1978) 446-85. On the Patmos/Rhodes discussions, consult A. de Halleux, "Inauguration du dialogue théologique officiel entre les Églises catholique et orthodoxe," *Revue théologique de Louvain* 11 (1980) 394-98.

June 6 and 7, 1981, an Orthodox/Roman Catholic prayer service at which Pope John Paul II, still recuperating from a gunshot wound, delivered a recorded message in which he prayed in Greek the original creedal symbol of Constantinople: "We believe in the Holy Spirit, the Lord and Giver of Life, who proceeds from the Father."

Our considerations have become all the more promising in light of the unprecedented, unanimous vote in Lima, Peru, on January 12, 1982, by 120 theologians and leaders of the Orthodox, Roman Catholic and Protestant churches in favor of accepting a major text on baptism, Eucharist, and ministry prepared by the Faith and Order Commission of the World Council of Churches. The texts in the words of the members have "been brought to such a stage of maturity that they are now ready for transmission to the churches." However, the official dialogue that is taking place between the Orthodox and Roman Catholic churches is bound to be difficult because of the centuries of separation.

What is Eastern Orthodoxy?

Who are the Eastern Orthodox? Custom dictates that we refer to *Eastern* Orthodox even though today many of their churches are not located only on the Eastern shores of the Mediterranean or in Middle Eastern countries. These Christian churches, now strongly represented also in Western countries, such as Canada, are basically churches whose roots reach down historically to the ancient sees of Jerusalem, Antioch, Alexandria, later Constantinople, and later still various sees such as Moscow and other Slavic centers. For over a millennium these churches and the Western churches were united in the one great and holy Undivided Church despite occasional tension and difficulties. It was in the East that Christianity had begun. Though Jesus and his disciples spoke Aramaic, the New Testament writings and most of the early preaching of the apostolic Church were spread, as you know, in Greek, the lingua franca of the first-century Mediterranean. Drawing partly upon religious terms of the Greek translation of the Hebrew Bible, the Septuagint, Greek speakers adapted the gospel for the non-Jewish world. Especially after the fall of Jerusalem and the decimation of the Jewish-Christian communities, Greek became all the more important; even in Rome bishops spoke Greek into the third century. In the East Christianity hosted the ecumenical councils of the first thousand years; in the East the eucharistic liturgies took their shape. After Emperor Constantine's transfer of the capital of the Roman Empire from the Old Rome to the new Rome, Byzantium, or Constantinople as he called it, became an important ecclesiastical see. The old Rome, because of its early hegemony, its wealth, its reputation for sound doctrine, its association with veneration of two illustrous martyrs, Peter and Paul, the role of moderation and conciliation assumed by the Roman bishops in early centuries, retained much of its prestige. Thus, for these first centuries, Mark Twain notwithstanding, East was West and West was East, and the churches in distinct sectors of the world experienced a harmonious symbiosis, without expecting rigid uniformity. Long before modern communication, the churches made their own decisions, remained in touch with one another through letters and visits.

As two distinctive languages, Greek and Latin, came to be used more and more in the churches, mutual understanding declined, suspicions mounted, different liturgical and administrative procedures developed. Fears of Western, especially papal, encroachment grew. Then, later in the Middle Ages, when crusades were organized supposedly only for liberating the holy places of Christianity from occupation by the infidels, some Western rulers used this occasion for trade benefits, self-aggrandizement, plundering, interference in Eastern countries and churches. There were even establishments of rival Latin patriarchates and monasteries. No wonder then that the East feared and resented the powerful West. In more recent times, the Eastern churches have had to contend with persecuting powers: the Turks, Muslim Arabs, Soviet Communists.

Still, despite persecution and dispersal, Orthodoxy today represents a vigorous and vibrant part of Christianity, a sister church to Roman Catholicism, with whom Orthodoxy now wishes to reestablish full communion if such can happen without compromising Orthodoxy's own convictions and characteristics.[2] Orthodoxy, deeply rooted in various national cultures, has kept alive a rich theological tradition and is in fact depository of much of the patrimony from the Great and Undivided Church. It has preserved ancient liturgies, venerated saintly Christians, created imaginative structures of church governance, produced distinctive religious art. But one special feature has been its appreciation of the integrity of the local churches, and the appropriateness of reaching decisions through consultations in synods. Yet Orthodoxy represents a form of Christianity that has never experienced the centralizing effects of the papacy as in Western Europe, even though Orthodoxy in the Byzantine Empire did see church and state, emperor, and patriarch,

---

[2] A useful contemporary assessment of Orthodoxy by a British Orthodox theologian is Kallistos Ware, *The Orthodox Way* (London, 1979).

wedded so closely as to threaten the Church's independence. Many Church Fathers, theologians of the Eastern churches, are part of the common patrimony of the Undivided Church, hailed as saints also in the liturgical calendars of the West: Basil of Caesarea, John Chrysostom, Gregory the Theologian, Cyril of Jerusalem, and many others. Amid churches so vast and independent, Orthodoxy, to be sure, has had problems in achieving consensus and cooperation. Likewise, as we have seen, Orthodoxy has been oppressed in various centuries through persecutions. Nonetheless, Orthodoxy is no museum piece; from it radiates a dynamic center of spiritual energy for the modern world.[3]

Orthodoxy in North America

Obviously we cannot here review centuries of Orthodox history, nor can we describe Orthodoxy as it flourished in various cultures. Instead we choose to focus especially on the Orthodox experience in North America. Here Protestants and Roman Catholics alike find the world of Orthodoxy mysterious and puzzling. Few, except through intermarriage, have direct contact with Eastern Orthodox churches in North America. Vague impressions abound. We Roman Catholics characterize the Orthodox in popular imagination as Christians who celebrate lengthy liturgies in ancient languages, whose priests may marry, who reject the world-wide jurisdiction of the Pope, but who maintain a sacramental system akin to that of Roman Catholicism. Few Canadians realize that in North America alone there are over five million Eastern Christians, of whom about four million are Orthodox, persons whose churches have been affected by the fact of emigration.

Several years ago during a visit to New York City the then Orthodox Patriarch of Antioch Elias IV remarked in a sermon that the future of Orthodoxy is to be found in America where there must be one Orthodox Church. Away from Turkish or Soviet spheres of influence American Orthodoxy has achieved much. Hence the understandable sense of frustration and distress that from the North American scene not a single Orthodox theologian was called to attend the Patmos/Rhodes meeting. Because they are, strictly speaking, part of the Constantinople Patriarchate or are enjoying independent canonical status (currently being

---

[3]See, *The Orthodox Church in the Ecumenical Movement. Documents and Statements 1902-1975*, ed. Constantin G. Patelos (Geneva, 1978). See also, Vasil B. Istavridis, "The Orthodox Churches in the Ecumenical Movement 1948-1968," in Harold E. Fey, *A History of the Ecumenical Movement*, Vol. 2: *1948-1968* (Philadelphia, 1970), pp. 287-310.

challenged by some) the Orthodox in North America had no direct access to the Patmos/Rhodes consultation. Hence the meetings were deprived of an articulate, contemporary voice of church life.

Members of the various Orthodox churches in North America have shown mature ecumenical leadership, overcoming natural linguistic and cultural tensions. When the Eastern Orthodox/Roman Catholic bilateral consultation began in the mid 1960s, Archbishop Iakovos, Archbishop of the Greek Archdiocese of North and South America, reflected on the pluralistic nature of North American society and commented: "Here we can conduct the dialogue free of the nationalistic pressure which would first have to be overcome in overwhelmingly Catholic countries like Spain or Italy or in a predominantly Orthodox country like Greece."

In my reflections, I would like to outline some highlights of the early history of the Orthodox churches in North America, especially the history of the Russian Orthodox and Greek Orthodox communities. After describing some of these historical influences in the previous and present centuries we will be better able to appreciate their collaboration among themselves and their hope to enter into closer dialogue with other churches, especially the Roman Catholic Church.

Russian Orthodox in Alaska

The advent of Eastern Orthodoxy to North American soil dates to the explorations of Russian traders who began arriving in the mid-eighteenth century.[4] The Russian explorers John Bering and Alexis Chirikov who sighted the coast line of Alaska in 1741 had several priests with them on board. On July 20, 1741, two priests among the companions, Ilarion Trusov and Ignaty Korirevsky, celebrated the Orthodox Divine Liturgy, the first ever in North America, aboard the ship *Saint Peter*. In the fifty years that followed the discoveries of Bering and Chirokov, Alaska seemed to have appeal for its hunting, fishing and fur trapping, but not as a locus for missionary activity. Given the rigors of existence in that far Northern climate it is not surprising that no permanent settlement was set up until 1784 when a village was founded near present-day Kodiak.

---

[4]On the history of Orthodoxy in North America, cf. *Orthodox America 1794-1976. Development of the Orthodox Church in America*, eds. C. J. Tarasar and J. H. Erickson (Syosset, NY, 1975). Also the Ph.D. dissertation prepared for the State University of New York in Buffalo, 1973 by Joseph Hayden, *Slavic Orthodox Christianity in the United States. From Culture Religion to Sectarian Church* (Ann Arbor, Mich.: University Microfilms, 1974). And, Vasile Hategan, *Fifty Years of the Romanian Orthodox Church in America* (Jackson, Mich., 1959).

Almost ten years later in 1793 Empress Catherine of Russia instructed the Metropolitan of St. Petersburg to recruit missionaries for the Alaskan colony. On December 25, 1793, eight monks left St. Petersburg on one of the longest missionary journeys in Orthodox history, over 7000 miles, to Kokiak, Alaska. One of the monks, Father Herman, who worked among the Alaskan natives, the Aleuts, for forty-three years, was canonized as a saint in 1970, the first Orthodox saint of North America.

To meet the pastoral needs of the local church, the Holy Synod of the Russian Church decided early to establish a missionary bishopric in Alaska and the Aleutian Islands. One of the eight original missionary monks, Ioasaf (Bolotov), was asked to return to Russia where in 1798 he was consecrated bishop of that missionary region, comprising Alaska and the islands. After his consecration, on his return to Alaska, he was tragically drowned at sea when his ship, the *Phoenix*, sank in a treacherous storm. After that accident, no bishop was appointed for forty years and Alaska remained under the jurisdiction of the Russian diocese of Irkutsk. In 1812 part of the Alaskan mission expanded into California where the chapel of Saint Helen was established at Fort Ross, California, approximately eighty miles north of San Francisco. This church remained open until 1841. Later in 1868 a parish was founded in San Francisco.

During this formative period in Alaskan missionary history one person in particular stands out, the priest John Veniaminov (1797-1879), later known as the Apostle of Alaska. Besides his preaching and teaching he became known for his scholarly activities which included translating parts of the Bible and the Divine Liturgy into the Aleut language. He also composed a native catechism. It was Veniaminov who was consecrated bishop (Innocent) of Kamchatka, a new see which would include in its territory the New Archangel (Sitka) mission. Thus in 1840 the American mission was removed from the diocese of Irkutsk. Bishop Innocent was active in this territory as a missionary for twenty-two years. In 1858 the bishopric of Sitka received the status of an auxiliary see to the Kamchatka diocese. With the sale of Alaska to the United States in 1867 Sitka became an independent missionary see.

In 1872 the Bishop's see was transferred from Sitka, Alaska, to San Francisco and received in 1900 the title Diocese of the Aleutian Islands and North America. Subsequently in 1905 the diocese was transferred again, this time to New York City, which became the headquarters of North America. Until 1917 the Eastern Orthodox Church of Russia was the only canonical representative at the episcopal level in the United States and Canada. After 1917 and the Russian revolution which brought a breakdown in communications between the United States and the

Patriarchate of Moscow, Russia was no longer able to exercise effective control over its North American establishment and this led to a shift in jurisdiction. In 1924 the Russian Diocese in America at its *sobor* (council) proclaimed a "temporary self-government." The American Russian community took for itself the name "Metropolia."

During the nineteenth century, as is well known, a large wave of immigration from Eastern and Southern European and Middle Eastern countries took place to the United States and Canada. From 1880 to the beginning of World War I nearly one million Eastern Christians immigrated to the U.S.A., one-half of whom were Orthodox, with Russians, Greeks, Syrians and Serbs predominating. These Orthodox left their own hierarchy behind in their native countries. On the basis of earlier precedents, it was argued that Orthodox, once in a new land, should come under the jurisdiction of that Orthodox church which had initiated missionary activity there, namely the successors to the Russian Orthodox mission community. However, the situation was to change dramatically beginning about 1920 among the Greek Orthodox.

Greek Orthodox Church in America

To understand the history of Orthodoxy in North America in this century it is important to look also at the origins and history of what is now the largest, most highly structured of all the North American Orthodox families, the Greek Orthodox Church in North America.[5] Greek Orthodox had not been strangers in the early years of the American colonies. Since 1767 there was a temporary Greek Orthodox community established at New Smyrna, Florida. Also, a hundred years later in 1864, came the establishment of the first Greek parish at New Orleans. Still, the situation of the Greek Orthodox community was bound to change with the influx of immigrants and with increasing construction of churches.

The ten years prior to World War I and the years up to 1921 were the key years for Greek immigration to North America. The number of immigrants from the Greek mainland and islands from 1903 to 1921 is said to have matched the number of immigrants from all other countries for those years. Most of these Greeks settled east of the Mississippi River

---

[5] See, John E. Rexine, "Fifty Years of the Greek Orthodox Archdiocese in America," *Diakonia*, 12 (1977) 189-91. A useful source of current activities of the Greek Orthodox Archdiocese of North and South America is its current *Yearbook*, published privately each year and available from 10 E. 79th St., New York, NY 10021.

and north of the Ohio. New England, New York and the Lake Michigan area were favorite locations. Chicago at one time was the third largest Greek-speaking city in the world after Athens and Thessalonike. Churches in the new wave were set up in New York City, Boston, Chicago and Montreal. By the year 1918 there were some 130 churches serving Greek Orthodox in the U.S.A.

In 1918 with the arrival from Greece of Bishop Meletios Metaxakis there was organized an archdiocese under the jurisdiction of Athens. This meant that an Orthodox ecclesiastical body, namely the Greek Orthodox Church in America, was now organized on a purely ethnic basis, and independent of the North American diocese stemming from the Alaskan mission. In 1921 Meletios was unexpectedly called to Constantinople to become the Ecumenical Patriarch. At the time of his installation as Patriarch he reflected in a speech upon his short stay in America and expressed the hope that some day the then two million Orthodox in North America would be organized into one "American Orthodox Church." But he established the Greek Archdiocese of America under his own direct jurisdiction, the Patriarchate of Constantinople, a situation which continues to this day.

That present arrangement of direct dependence is not without its inconveniences for the Greek Orthodox in North America and has increased the difficulties that faced Orthodox attempts at collaboration. Despite a series of remarkable leaders, two of whom went on to become ecumenical patriarchs, Meletios and Athenagoras (Archbishop in the Americas from 1930-1949), the enormous size of the Greek Archdiocese—literally all of North and South America—makes it difficult to administer. Furthermore, the vitality and creativity of the North American Orthodox community is consistently underrepresented at the international Orthodox consultations and meetings simply because, strictly speaking, the community is part of the Ecumenical Patriarchate. A typical example of this was the small American Orthodox delegation, merely two theologians, at the first Pre-Conciliar Panorthodox Conference, held at Chambésy, Switzerland, in November 1976. Not surprisingly, one of the agenda items for the forthcoming Pan-Orthodox Synod which intensely concerns the North American Orthodox is the question of autocephaly and independent national churches.

The present incumbent of the Greek Orthodox Archdiocese of North and South America is Archbishop Iakovos (Coucouzes) who was installed in that office in 1959. He is doubtless one of the most well-known Orthodox hierarchs in the Americas today. Singlehandedly he has influenced ecumenical relations with other Christians. Archbishop

Iakovos, the first American citizen to hold this office, was born in 1911 on the island of Imbros, part of Turkey's possessions today. He had an excellent theological formation beginning in the Orthodox school at Halki, and then at Harvard University. His experience as a teacher and more especially his activities at the World Council of Churches in Geneva where he was the personal representative of the Ecumenical Patriarchate from 1955 to 1959 have been of capital importance. In addition to his theological and ecumenical expertise he brings an effective pastoral sense to inter-church discussions. His concern for social justice and human rights dates back to the earliest days of the civil rights movement.[6] In addition to his responsibility for over two million Greek Orthodox, he assumed leadership in discussion among American Orthodox which led to the ultimate formation in 1960 of the Standing Conference of Canonical Bishops in the Americas (SCOBA) which has striven to eliminate ethnic and cultural rivalries and suspicions among the Orthodox of different backgrounds.[7] If the Greek Orthodox community gives the appearance of being more actively involved ecumenically in North America than other Orthodox communities this is doubtless due to the personal encouragement of Archbishop Iakovos himself.

Under the theological direction of Rev. Dr. Robert Stephanopoulos, a graduate of Holy Cross and of Boston University's School of Theology and a member of the Greek Orthodox Archdiocese, SCOBA published in 1973 an impressive study entitled *Guidelines for Orthodox Christians in Ecumenical Relations.*[8] Although somewhat cautious and conservative, especially on the feasibility of Eucharistic hospitality or intercommunion and on the question of what constitutes full church membership, still the guidelines are a splendid example of joint Orthodox commitment to

---

[6] As typical of the social and doctrinal concerns of the Greek Orthodox hierarchy, see the collection: *Encyclicals and Documents of the Greek Orthodox Archdiocese of North and South America Relating to its Thought and Activity: The First Fifty Years (1922-1972),* ed. D. J. Constantelos (Thessalonike, 1976).

[7] On the development of SCOBA and the structural organization of the various Orthodox churches in North America, see the valuable work by Arthur Carl Piepkorn, *Profiles in Belief. The Religious Bodies of the United States and Canada,* Volume 1: *Roman Catholic, Old Catholic, Eastern Orthodox* (New York, 1977), pp. 61-116.

[8] *Guidelines for Orthodox Christians in Ecumenical Relations,* published by the Standing Conference of Canonical Orthodox Bishops in America (SCOBA), written by R. G. Stephanopoulos (New York, 1973). Stephanopoulos, an Orthodox priest who graduated from Boston University with a Ph.D. in theology, has written an unpublished dissertation, *A Study in Recent Greek Orthodox Ecumenical Relations 1902-1968* (Boston University, Ph.D. 1970). See also his, "Reflections on Orthodox Ecumenical Directions after Uppsala," *Journal of Ecumenical Studies,* 9 (1972) 301-17.

ecumenism.[9] It is a pity that this document is not widely known outside of North America. The guidelines note that "the true spirit of ecumenism, compatible with Orthodox principles and particulars, should be developed through education in the home, the Church and the schools." It further recommends ecumenical perspectives in official clergy conferences, in theological workshops, and at university campuses. Also expressed is a strong commitment to conversations with other Christian churches, willingness to continue cooperation with the World Council of Churches, the National Council of Churches, and other regional and local councils. The document contains some features that one might wish to see expanded, especially what is said about the role of laypeople in the church, the feasibility of eventual intercommunion, the possibility of responsible innovations. But what is said is far in advance over much that comes from Orthodox countries, especially the Church of Greece. Also notable are its suggestions regarding social problems and issues of our day such as social change, peace, justice and human development. The guidelines offer several suggested forms of common prayer for ecumenical services. Appended to the guidelines is a collection of pertinent international Orthodox ecumenical documents clearly meant to give added weight to the American proposals.

The Autocephaly of the "Orthodox Church in America"

As we have seen, what was formally known as the Russian Orthodox Church of America, or Metropolia, that group of Orthodox communicants who traced their history to the mission of the monks in Alaska in 1794, had at first moved toward temporary independent status because of the Russian Revolution and the interruptions of the World Wars, a fact not appreciated at first by the Synod of the Orthodox Church in Russia. For many years, especially under the inspiration and encouragement of faculty members at St. Vladimir's Theological School in New York, plans were drawn up to organize and to petition for "autocephalous" or independent status from the Mother Church in Russia. This was a sensitive issue within the Greek Orthodox Archdiocese which felt that negotiations of such importance should be discussed and approved not in Moscow but by the Ecumenical Patriarch in Constantinople.[10]

---

[9] Philip Timko, "Orthodox Ecclesiology and Ecumenical Practice: Guidelines for Orthodox Christians in Ecumenical Relations," *Worship*, 50 (1976) 137-45.

[10] *St. Vladimir's Theological Quarterly*, 15, 1-2, (1971) devoted its entire double issue to the history and reasons for the Russian Orthodox Church in America's application for autocephalous status from the Moscow patriarchate. In that issue see especially the contribution of the senior Orthodox theologian Alexander Schmemann, "A Meaningful

Finally, plans went ahead over protests and on April 10, 1970, Alexis, patriarch of Moscow, with the approval of the Synod of the Russian Orthodox Church, granted the American Metropolia the status of being the Autocephalous Orthodox Church in America. The text or "Tomos" was signed by Patriarch Alexis who died only six days later on April 16, 1970. An official delegation from North America, led by Bishop Theodosius, arrived in Moscow to accept the official "Tomos" from the Guardian of the Throne, Metropolitan Pimen on May 18, 1970. At a meeting held in Montreal in 1976, Bishop Theodosius subsequently was elected Metropolitan of what is now known as the Orthodox Church of America (OCA).

At the same time the decree of the Russian patriarch established the OCA as an instrument of unity for all Orthodox Christians in America. It invited all national Orthodox jurisdictions in America to join in unity with the OCA. Needless to say, this invitation was greeted with less than enthusiasm especially by the Greek Orthodox who were larger and already better organized structurally.[11] Despite many months of shock and grief that the OCA had taken such a unilateral step, the Orthodox community at large weathered this serious crisis, although the memory of the *fait accompli* is never far removed. What Alexander Schmemann described as "a meaningful storm," namely the declaration of autocephaly, has not completely abated on the American scene. Much theological literature has appeared as a result.

The Two Major Orthodox Traditions in North America

Perhaps some will feel it inappropriate for a Roman Catholic to indulge in any kind of judgments about the two strong Orthodox communities in North America, the "Russian" branch in the OCA, and the "Greek" branch in the Archdiocese. In spiritual matters no one can judge except by one's own limited perception. What one observes remains necessarily impressionistic and phenomenological. Also, one tends to judge an entire community by positions, actions and attitudes of the Orthodox hierarchies or clergy which is of course not the only source for measuring the religious atmospheric pressure. Still some reports can be made to help the outsider

---

Storm: Some Reflections on Autocephaly Tradition and Ecclesiology," *Saint Vladimir's Theological Quarterly*, 15 (1971) 3-27. See also Archimandrite Seraphim (Surrency), *The Quest for Orthodox Church Unity in America, A History of the Orthodox Church in North America in the Twentieth Century* (New York, 1973).

[11] Panagiotes N. Trempelas, *The Autocephaly of the Metropolia in America*, trans. and ed. G. S. Bebis et al. (Brookline, Mass., 1973).

interpret what is taking place in American Orthodoxy.

Part of the genius of Orthodox church polity is its great emphasis on the importance of the local church, the eucharistic community par excellence. This theological emphasis helps Orthodoxy absorb tensions with greater facility than is often possible for instance in Roman Catholicism. In Orthodoxy today, particularly in North America, a delicate situation such as the one Catholicism has had to contend with, Archbishop Lefebvre's traditionalism, would probably be resolved with greater flexibility and compromise. Members of the OCA and Greek Orthodox and other Orthodox members are able to remain in contact and dialogue despite ruffled feelings and occasional angry outbursts.

It seems true to say that the Orthodox Church in America (OCA) has in recent years been less culturally identified with any specific ethnic group than is the case with the Greek Orthodox. The OCA is perceived as generally adapting more rapidly to the American religious scene. Christians in North America who are drawn to enter into communion with the Orthodox church will normally find it easier to feel at home in the OCA. In previous years in America this group of Orthodox was able to draw heavily upon a rich theological tradition developed in Russia during a period when the Greek church was struggling for survival against the Turks. Much of the Russian theological insights came to America from émigré theologians who had settled first at the Theological Institute of St. Sergius in Paris. This center for higher Orthodox studies in exile was founded after the Russian Revolution and has formed some of the Orthodox intelligentsia now living in the United States.

Both Orthodox communities, those whose roots were originally Russian or Greek, are deeply dedicated to adapting Orthodox life to its new setting in America. Today both of these communities have a limited number of theologians, priests or laymen. Demands made on their time and energy are unrealistically numerous. Priest-theologians in addition to their teaching and writing are responsible for administering parishes. Orthodox communities have been committed for many years in America to publishing high-quality journals such as the *St. Vladimir's Theological Quarterly* and *The Greek Orthodox Theological Review.* Serious theological education for clergy, and more recently for laity, receives high priority. More and more young scholars among the Orthodox are taking degrees in American universities.

Because the Greeks have easier access to their home country some tend to do at least some of their graduate studies in Greece. Some students from Greece do their seminary studies in the U.S.A., thus giving the institution some connection with the country of origin. Seminarians however at St. Vladimir's Seminary have far less knowledge, if any, of the Russian language today than is the case with Greek Orthodox students at the Holy Cross Greek Orthodox School of Theology. This difference in command of the languages is reflected too in the celebration of the Divine Liturgy. English is much more common at liturgical prayer in the OCA divinity school than it is among the Greek Orthodox at prayer in their school of theology.

Orthodox Schools of Theology in North America

To understand Orthodox life in North America today it is crucial to be acquainted with at least the two principal schools of theology which train and form future American Orthodox clergy and religious educators. Greek Orthodox theological education in the United States did not begin with the establishment of the Holy Cross School of Theology, as is often incorrectly presumed. As early as 1921 in Astoria, New York, the Greeks opened St. Athanasios Seminary for the formation of priests. Unfortunately it had to close its doors after only two years of operation. The problems were largely financial, as it was difficult to solicit funds from the Greek community who tended to regard themselves as only temporarily in the United States until political and economic matters were settled in their home country.

However, on September 15, 1937, under the urging of Archbishop Athenagoras who later became the Ecumenical Patriarch of Constantinople, a theological seminary was opened in the rural setting of Pomfret, Connecticut. Fifteen young candidates for ordination entered the seminary that year. The seminary was directed by its first dean, Archimandrite (later Archbishop) Athenagoras Cavadas. The name given to the center of learning was the Holy Cross Greek Orthodox School of Theology. In its early years the seminary was really a preparatory school, comprising courses of two years duration after which it was envisaged that students would move on either to Athens or Halki for theological studies proper. This two-year program was expanded at first into a four-year and then a five-year course, partly because of the restrictions on travel caused by World War II.

In 1946 the Greek Orthodox Seminary moved from Pomfret to a new home in suburban Boston, its present location in Brookline. This setting enabled its faculty and students to share in the wealth of educational centers in the greater Boston area. In 1976 the first Greek Orthodox layman was appointed president of this Holy Cross School of Theology, Dr. Thomas Lelon. In the same year the Maliotis Cultural Center was opened which also became the setting for the annual Patriarch Athenagoras Memorial Lectures. An important Orthodox publishing house was established in Brookline and numerous works, either original or translated from Greek, were made available to the reading public.

Recently the Holy Cross Greek Orthodox School of Theology entered into full membership with the Boston Theological Institute, an ecumenical consortium of theological schools. This new association helped the seminarians to enter more fully into the pattern of American theological education and introduced them into typical American institutions such as "field education" as a supplement to formal theological studies. Understandably, there remained shyness and isolation among some of the Orthodox seminarians as they entered into direct contact with Roman Catholic and Protestant communities, but this feeling has been disappearing more and more. The first woman to receive a graduate degree of theology did so in 1976. The following year three more women graduated, trained especially as religious educators. The current student body includes students from the U.S.A. and Canada, but also from Greece, Jordan, Korea, and Uganda.

The Russian Orthodox community in North America operates a similar school which has a parallel history. St. Vladimir's Seminary opened in 1938 in New York City. The first students were accomodated in apartments located at the Protestant Union Theological Seminary in upper Manhattan. In the mornings the students attended university classes at nearby Columbia University and in the afternoons heard lectures in theology at the parish hall of Christ the Savior parish in New York. The following year a temporary home was found for them on the campus of the Episcopal General Theological Seminary.

As with many other American centers of learning the war years were difficult ones financially. From 1938 to 1948 the seminary was in precarious existence. To many of the immigrant Orthodox the notion of a college degree for its future clergy seemed an unnecessary luxury. But the idea eventually caught on and enrollments increased. In 1948 St. Vladimir's was reorganized as a theological academy (the Russian equivalent of a graduate school of theology). Its faculty boasted many prestigious figures of Russian Orthodox theology including Georges Florovsky, Nicholas Arsenieff, Nicholas Lossky, Alexander Schmemann, and Serge Verkhovsky.

In 1962 the seminary was relocated in Crestwood, New York, in residential Westchester County, about one hour north of New York City. The new location provided a better setting for its library which numbered some 35,000 volumes of Orthodox theology. The new setting is also the site of the publication of *St. Vladimir's Theological Quarterly*, and a publishing house which makes available in translation important works of theology.

Orthodox Theologians in North America Today

Although many Orthodox theologians residing in America were trained in European universities and academies, their publications today reflect their involvement in a new setting. One of the senior members of the American theological community was the late Georges Florovsky, born in Odessa in 1893, who was professor in Odessa, Prague and Paris before moving to the United States. After teaching at St. Vladimir's from 1948-1955 he was invited to become professor of Eastern Church History at Harvard Divinity School from 1956 until his retirement in 1964. Four volumes of his collected works have recently been published as well as a commemorative volume in his honor in 1975.[12] Two other Orthodox theologians are well known for their publications: Alexander Schmemann[13] and John Meyendorff. The latter has written widely especially on the theological system of Saint Gregory Palamas and Byzantine Hesychasm. His *Byzantine Theology: Historical Trends and Doctrinal Themes* (1974) is a respected interpretation of contemporary Orthodox thought. Two other professors from St. Vladimir's are earning high marks for their research: Fr. Thomas Hopko and John Erickson, a lay theologian who has specialized in canon law and the history of the important term "economy" in Eastern thought.

At the Holy Cross Greek Orthodox School of Theology in Brookline, a distinguished faculty of theology has published works in Greek and English. Special mention should be made of the Louvain-trained Maximos Aghiorgoussis, now Bishop of Pittsburgh, as well as Stanley Harakas, Theodore Stylianopoulos, N. Michael Vaporis, George Bebis, and Lewis Patsavos (the last two of whom are laymen). Other North American Orthodox scholars who are well known include Deno Geanakoplos, professor of Byzantine history at Yale University and Demetrios Constantelos, professor at Stockton State College, Pomona, New Jersey. One drawback to the publications of North American Orthodox writers

---

[12] See *Collected Works of G. Florovsky*, 4 vols., available from the Nordland Publishing Co., Belmont, Mass. A special *Festschrift* appeared in 1975 to honor this scholar: *Heritage of the Early Church*. Essays in Honor of G. V. Florovsky, ed. D. Neimann and M. Schatkin, *Orientalia Christiana Analecta*, 195 (Rome, 1975).

[13] Father Schmemann died on December 13, 1983.

is that they are not widely distributed; the non-Orthodox reader needs to survey attentively Orthodox journals and booklists to keep abreast of recent publications.

Orthodox Ecumenical Activity in North America

Despite nationalistic rivalries, tensions, and jurisdictional controversies among the Orthodox communities in America, the Orthodox churches have carried out especially since 1960 a number of important ecumenical dialogues with Roman Catholics, Anglicans, Protestants, and more recently with the Jewish community.[14] The North American setting has been ideal for such dialogues since here Old World suspicions and antagonisms are far less pronounced than in Europe and the Middle East.

In the context of this lecture, we can concentrate only on the official bilateral conversations in North America that have been underway with Roman Catholics since 1965.[15] From a Canadian perspective one would have to note the absence of Canadian input into these dialogues because Orthodoxy's headquarters are located in the U.S.A., and the Catholics are chosen by the United States Catholic Conference, not the Canadian Conference of Catholic Bishops. These dialogues are unique in their genre for the world. Fifteen years before the Patmos/Rhodes encounter these meetings have been taking place twice each year and have to date produced eight agreed statements concerning topics such as: the Eucharist, mixed marriages, respect for life, the Church, pastoral office of bishops and priests, ecclesiastical "economy," the sanctity of marriage, and the spiritual formation of children. The consensus statements, although not intended to be fully developed theological treatises, are helpful pastoral guidelines suggesting how the churches might deal with questions sometimes hotly disputed in the past. These statements cannot be analyzed with the same presuppositions one would use to assess consensus

---

[14] On international and North American Orthodox ecumenical consultations, see, N. Ehrenström and G. Gassmann, *Confessions in Dialogue. A Survey of Bilateral Conversations among World Confessional Families 1959-1974*, 3rd rev. ed. (Geneva, 1975). Lists of Orthodox conversations with Roman Catholics in North America (pp. 117-20), with Anglicans (pp. 57-60), with Lutherans (pp. 89-90), with Reformed (pp. 113-15), with Lutherans and Reformed (p. 91). See also the volume prepared by the WCC, *Orthodox Church and the Churches of the Reformation. A Survey of Orthodox-Protestant Dialogues*, Faith and Order Commission, Faith and Order Paper no. 76 (Geneva, 1975).

[15] A recent analysis of the Eastern Orthodox/Roman Catholic dialogue in the U.S.A., together with the texts of the agreed statements, is: Edward J. Kilmartin, *Toward Reunion: The Orthodox and Roman Catholic Churches* (New York, 1979).

statements between Western (Catholic and Protestant) churches. When in fact a research committee of the Catholic Theological Society of America used such criteria to assess these published statements they could only judge them to be "most disappointing." This assessment failed to take into account the historical importance of Orthodox and Roman Catholic theologians being able to agree to "our remarkable and fundamental agreement" and "our common Christian tradition." The statements may be laconic but the forthrightness and conviction of the statements are quite unique in modern-day Orthodox/Roman Catholic exchange. Given the history of separateness between the two traditions it is amazing that the theologians could agree: "our two traditions of viewing the Church are not easily harmonized yet we believe the Spirit is ever active to show us the way by which we can live together as one and many."

Currently, I consider there are ten critical areas in theology that cause tension between Eastern Orthodox and Roman Catholic churches: (1) The conceptions accorded theology itself by East and West, apophatic theology vs. kataphatic theology, or theology inspired by Scripture, the Fathers, the Conciliar and synodal canons vs. theology inspired by Scripture, the Fathers, the synods, Scholasticism and recent philosophic perspectives; (2) the identification of how we reach knowledge about the Three-in-One God both now and in eternal life, especially as reflected in the Palamite theology of essence and energies; (3) the identification and interpretation of ecumenical councils (though here even the Roman Catholic Papacy has begun to categorize councils into two classes: the ecumenical synods of the great and Undivided Church, and the general councils of the West, including Trent, Vatican I and II); (4) the Petrine ministry in the Church and its relationship to the Papacy and the Ecumenical Patriarchate; (5) the meaning to attach to Eastern Catholic churches, those churches sometimes disparingly referred to as Uniate; (6) the nature of the local eucharistic community as embodiment of the whole church, that is, eucharistic ecclesiology; (7) the grounds for approving and forbidding intercommunion or eucharistic hospitality; (8) the theology of marriage; (9) the meaning and structure of ordained ministry in the church (including the function of deacons, presbyters, the ordination of women); (10) the role of liturgy, sacred art and prayer.

By way of illustration I wish to point to several suggestions or judgments stated in the recent Orthodox/Roman Catholic consensus statements in North America on Eucharist, Church, pastoral office, and mixed marriages.

(a) *The Eucharist:* The joint statement on the Eucharist confirms what is generally recognized by theologians that there is no basic disagreement between Orthodox and Roman Catholics regarding the celebration of the Eucharist. But the consultation recognized that more is required than this unity of belief before it is possible to hold regular eucharistic sharing or intercommunion. It noted that the unity of love that covers the range of essentials of Christian life, or, to use the expression of Vatican II, "full communion," is not yet sufficiently realized between Catholics and Orthodox to warrant regular eucharistic sharing. Questions such as the meaning of transubstantiation or the sanctification of the eucharistic elements by the Holy Spirit, the so-called "epiclesis," are not treated in the text since they are perceived to be theological rather than dogmatic questions. The published text does stress the necessity of the bishop or presbyter for the proper celebration of the Eucharist.

(b) *The Church:* Another statement, this one on the nature of the Church, stressed that its prototype lies within the blessed Trinity where both the distinction and unity of persons are based on love. Hence, it is reasoned, the Church is called to reflect on the fact that its unity is based on love and not on external law. The Church's continuity with its origins is grounded on the source of love in the Church which is the Holy Spirit. Here the Spirit's presence is described as being visibly expressed in historical forms such as Sacred Scripture, the sacraments, and ministry ordained in apostolic succession. Since these historical forms are found in the local church, the community gathered around the bishop and other ministers is truly Church. The local church's independent existence is considered splendidly expressed in the eucharistic celebration where Church is manifested and realized. At the same time the local church is seen as dependent upon other local churches which also possess the same Spirit of Christ. Within this interdependence of churches there is recognized a communion of churches which does not however exclude the fundamental equality of all churches. The nature of papal primacy is described as the central contested issue separating the sister churches of Orthodoxy and Catholicism.

(c) *Pastoral office:* The common statement prepared by the Orthodox and Catholic theologians concerning pastoral office begins with a historical section highlighting the gradual growth in understanding regarding the role of bishops and presbyters that has occurred in the Church. After a list of eight theological elements of agreement, the consensus report then enumerates in summary form those most hotly disputed questions. Here it is noted that within Roman Catholic theology some have questioned the affirmation that seems to be commonly asserted by Catholic and Orthodox traditions that pastoral office "directly represents" Christ. Some theologians, it continues, would hold that a pastor (bishop or priest) "directly represents" the faith of the Church and thereby also represents Christ who is the source of the Church's faith. Some Roman Catholic theologians, it observes, differ with the traditional Orthodox and Catholic affirmations by arguing that women could be ordained to the office of bishop or presbyter, if the Church were to authorize this decision. On the question of life-style for clerics, it is stated that pastoral ministry is compatible with occupations not directly associated with it, as the practice of the Church has shown. The relationship of celibacy to pastoral office is seen as a problem both for Orthodox and Roman Catholics. The statement also notes that while the question of married bishops and marriage after ordination is being raised in the Orthodox church, the issue of celibacy in the Roman Catholic church of the Roman rite is focused on the advisability of committing pastoral office to the married.

(d) *Mixed Marriages:* The Orthodox/Roman Catholic consultation has discussed several distinct issues related to marriage: the indissolubility of marriage; weddings between Orthodox and Catholics; the official minister of the sacrament of marriage; the sacramental nature of marriage; pastoral care of those who are divorced or in a troubled marriage; and finally, the spiritual formation of children from mixed marriages. The possibility of divorce and remarriage after a sacramental marriage is perceived differently by Orthodox and Catholic practices. The text published on this subject agrees that in Christian marriage a human situation is taken up into the life of faith; hence marriage partners have a vocation to live their marriage so that it might be seen as a type of the relation that exists between Christ and his Church (Eph 5.31-35) and thus also as a witness to the world of God's love for all humankind.

Some progress was made in the agreement about pastoral care of persons entering a "mixed marriage." The consultation held the position that the couple themselves should make the decision regarding the specific tradition in which children will receive religious training, after parents have consulted both Orthodox and Catholic pastors. Furthermore, in the agreed statement, the somewhat surprising opinion is proposed that marriages between Orthodox and Catholics should normally take place before an Orthodox priest, based on the fact that the Orthodox traditionally view the priest as the minister of the sacrament. The Orthodox theologians have difficulty in recognizing how a Catholic priest who considers himself only the official witness of the Church at a wedding would have sufficient intention to fulfill what is his proper attention. The consultation does note though that the Orthodox theology about who is the minister of marriage is not of ancient origin since in the first millennium of the great and Undivided Church marriages before civil magistrates were recognized as Christian marriages.

In the matter of pastoral care for the divorced the consultation is concerned with the healing process whereby pastors help these Christians enter more fully into the life of the Christian community. The consultation is aware of writings that note that psychological immaturity sometimes leads persons to exercise poor judgment in the choice of a marriage partner.

These are only some of the issues that have been addressed in a pastoral and theological way. The consultation hopes that what it has already published will receive wide attention in the local churches and that further clarifications can be published.

International Dialogue

What now of dialogue among the Orthodox and Roman Catholics on a more international scale? Many hopes are linked to an eventual convocation of a proposed Pan-Orthodox Great and Holy Council that many hope will take place in the coming years.[16] This event which could be compared to a general council such as Vatican II was long the dream of the late Ecumenical Patriarch Athenagoras. In 1968 among the various independent Orthodox churches he achieved majority support for the convocation of a synod of all Orthodoxy at a date to be determined. In 1972 an Interorthodox Preparatory Commission published a tentative working paper which was later revised at Chambésy, Switzerland, in 1976. The newer agenda for the Great and Holy Council focuses on ten topics, including questions related to the independence of national churches, adaptation to contemporary life, ecumenical relations with other churches. Currently some items such as revision of the Divine Liturgy are not on the agenda but it is hoped they may be added later.

From all international quarters there is general recognition that Roman Catholics and Orthodox face several important issues that need to be resolved before full communion can again be re-established. Here we list

---

[16] An initial description of the proposed Council can be found in *Towards the Great Council, Introductory Reports of the Interorthodox Commission in Preparation for the Next Great and Holy Council of the Orthodox Church* (London,1972). For more recent developments see, John Panagopoulos, "The Orthodox Church Prepares for the Council," *One in Christ*, 13 (1977) 229-37; Ion Bria, "L'espoir du Grand Synode orthodoxe," *Revue théologique de Louvain*, 8 (1977) 51-54.

only four such items.

Of major concern is the question of papal primacy and infallibility. One of the reasons why there was puzzlement and disappointment even among the Orthodox at the time of Hans Küng's rebuke by the Vatican was that he was seen as raising questions about papal infallibility and governance that, in its own way, Orthodoxy also wishes to raise. Theologians who are active in ecumenical dialogue with the Orthodox or Roman Catholics are in agreement that a clearer, more nuanced formulation of the function of papal primacy especially in the Western Catholic Church and a more modest description of papal infalliblility within the context of the Holy Spirit's fidelity to the Church are sorely needed.

Another question confronting Orthodox and Roman Catholic dialogue is the famous *Filioque* controversy.[17] As is well known, the Nicene-Constantinopolitan creed stated that the Holy Spirit "proceeds from [God] the Father." To that creed the West added a word that confesses that the Spirit proceeds from the Father *and from the Son (Filioque)*. This addition, as is now recognized, was motivated by a Western concern to highlight the divinity of the Son, Jesus Christ, especially in settings where Arianism was making inroads. Some theologians and church historians in the West now recognize that the addition of the phrase may have been ill-advised since, however well-intentioned the formula, it was perceived by the East as a flagrant violation of an agreement never to add to the creed, and that the action was never sanctioned at an ecumenical council. Through the historical studies that have appeared in the last several decades it is clear that the *Filioque* controversy is not an insurmountable obstacle for harmony between East and West. The difficulty could be solved by a quiet agreement of the West to omit the addition without having to deny the correctness of the affirmation. Or East and West could agree mutually to accept different formulations which would reflect simply different theological emphases rather than differences of belief.

Closer to home and more practical is the question of the relationship between the Orthodox Christians and the Eastern Catholic

---

[17] For recent studies on the *Filioque* controversy, see the articles by Michael Fahey (pp. 15-22) and T. Stylianopoulos (pp. 23-30), in *Conflicts About the Holy Spirit*, ed. Hans Küng and Jürgen Moltmann, *Concilium*, no. 128 [American edition] (New York, 1979) and *Spirit of God, Spirit of Christ: Ecumenical Reflections on the Filioque Controversy*, ed. L. Vischer (London, 1981).

churches.[18] Until recently the term "Uniates" was commonly employed to identify those Eastern Christian churches who had entered into communion with Rome. The term is now generally avoided and considered polemic and uncomplimentary. Of course each of these Eastern Catholic churches has had a distinctive history. Some had roots in Orthodoxy first before moving toward communion with Rome. Earlier statements from the Vatican sometimes gave the impression that the particular odyssey of the Eastern Catholic churches was meant to be a paradigm of how the Orthodox should enter "the mother church." The situation was further complicated by the fact that when these Eastern Christians entered into communion with Rome some of their distinctive liturgical and administrative traditions often suffered from a subtle process of Romanization. In other words, their legitimate, diverse traditions were lost by attrition or by Roman interference. For Orthodoxy the Uniate problem became a symbol of Roman, Western interference into the freedom of local churches.

Even at Vatican II there appeared a mild inconsistency relative to the Eastern Catholics and the Orthodox. In the conciliar decree on Eastern Catholic churches, *Orientalium ecclesiarum,* the Orthodox were invited to "join themselves to the unity of the Catholic Church" (no. 25), whereas in the decree on ecumenism, *Unitatis redintegratio,* Orthodox churches are referred to as "sister churches" (no. 14). This mild inconsistency would seem to imply that in one place the "Uniate" churches are considered almost as "bridge churches," yet, one might ask, why are bridge churches necessary if Orthodox churches are already sister churches?

This long simmering source of tension recently re-emerged toward the eve of the Patmos/Rhodes meeting. Two appointed Orthodox delegates representing the Church of Greece announced plans to boycott the ecumenical meeting with the Roman Catholics because the Catholic delegation was to include members of the Eastern Catholic churches. Orthodox Metropolitan Chrysostomos (Gerasimos) Zaphiris published a scathing article in the Greek theological journal, *Theologia,* in which he attacked the Uniates on a series of points.[19] Another Greek Orthodox delegate, Professor J. Karmiris, a conservative lay theologian, threatened

---

[18] On the relationship of the United Eastern Catholic churches and the Orthodox, see Emmanuel Lanne, "United Churches or Sister Churches: A Choice to be Faced," *One in Christ,* 12 (1976) 106-23.

[19] "A Problem and an Appeal: A Necessary Presupposition for the Beginning and the Success of the Theological Dialogue between the Orthodox and the Roman Catholic Churches," (in Greek) Θεολογία, 50 (1979) 856-68.

to resign from the official dialogue for the same reason. Eventually by a deft public statement published at the meeting which noted that the presence of the "Uniates" did not imply total Orthodox acceptance of their *raison d'être,* the threatened boycott was averted.

One doctrinal and disciplinary question that will confront Orthodox and Catholics in the coming years concerns the teaching about the indissolubility of marriage. The Orthodox share with the West a common vision of the sanctity and sacramentality of marriage, especially the view that marriage is a sign of Christ's devotion to his Church. However, according to an old tradition, the Orthodox church out of consideration for the human realities, permits divorces after it has exhausted all possible means to save the marriage. In fact, the Orthodox permit remarriages in order to avoid further human tragedies. This differs from the Roman Catholic procedure of dealing with unsuccessful marriages which shows its concern for the failed marriages by setting up an inquiry to uncover whether there may have existed some initial defect in the marriage bond or covenant which would in fact render the marriage null and void. If the Catholic Church perceives a defect it sees itself within its powers to declare an annulment that states in effect that no sacramental covenant existed. By this procedure the parties are then free to enter a marriage subsequently. The differences that exist between Orthodox and Roman Catholics in pastoral practice regarding the divorced, in the relative weight assigned to certain New Testament passages about divorce and their exegesis, and finally the differences in canonical legislation are all notable. But frank discussion between the two churches will surely help both East and West to understand better the different ecclesial traditions and how they can coexist in harmony.

The Future

As we approach now the third millennium it is no secret that Roman Catholics need to confess before God their numerous imperfections, institutional failings, their pride, thoughtlessness, and other sins. In a post-Vatican II period one cannot be shocked to hear that the church is a sinful church. Critics inside and outside the Orthodox church point to failures too in Eastern Christianity both in the North American setting and in other international settings. Orthodox will surely admit these and those failures of which they are personally quite aware. They will not feel obliged to reject out of hand the objections that they are often narrow in their interpretation of church history, hesitant to adopt practices that are not already authorized by ancient canons. They will recognize, as

Roman Catholics must do in certain countries, that there is sometimes a temptation to identify ethnic customs with religious necessities. Orthodox will want to respond to the objection that they suffer from excessive clericalism, specifically episcopalism, assigning almost exclusive authority to bishops. Amid theologians there has already begun a debate about whether or not the Orthodox concentrate too much on one particular theological tradition, such as the Hesychast theology of Saint Gregory Palamas (1296-1359), instead of drawing upon the vast richness of a broader history.[20] Catholics who have seen the overdominance of the theology and method of Saint Thomas Aquinas will understand the importance of this debate.

In North America the tremendous potential for Roman Catholics and Orthodox alike to advance towards better mutual understanding and cooperation already exists.[21] Many of the psychological barriers that have separated East and West are beginning to crumble on this continent. Now what is needed is greater grass roots involvement in this work of exchange and sharing. Among Canadian contributions to this exchange one can point to the role of the Pontifical Institute of Mediaeval Studies which in recent years has appointed several young scholars in the field of Byzantine theology and philosophy and in Medieval Russian history and literature.

In this new setting Orthodoxy is developing special, distinctive accents and expertise that enrich the international scene. One such example would be the kind of studies undertaken by Harakas in the U.S.A. concerning church and state theory and the American democratic tradition from an Orthodox perspective.[22] Already Catholic writers have shown an opening up of horizon thanks to their contact with North American Orthodox. Further developments will multiply as Orthodoxy prepares its agenda for the forthcoming Pan-Orthodox Great and Holy Council.

What we have described of Orthodox life and ecumenism is clearly only chapter one in a book still to be written. Is it utopian to dream that efforts now underway will lead to greater visible unity within this century? Perhaps in this century Orthodox and Roman Catholics will be free to

---

[20] See, Michael A. Fahey and John Meyendorff, *Trinitarian Theology East and West: St. Thomas Aquinas and St. Gregory Palamas* (Brookline, Mass., 1977).

[21] On the impact of Catholic and Orthodox dialogues today, see Michael A. Fahey, "Reconciliation Between Orthodoxy and Catholics: A Roman Catholic View," *Diakonia* [New York], 10 (1975) 4-23; and by the same author, "Ecclesiastical 'Economy' and Mutual Recognition of Faith: A Roman Catholic Perspective," *Diakonia*, 11 (1976) 204-23.

[22] Stanley Harakas, "Orthodox Church-State Theory and American Democracy," *The Greek Orthodox Theological Review*, 21 (1976) 399-421.

celebrate together in a common eucharistic liturgy, to accept each other in love as Church even to the point of pledging not to remold the others into their own image and likeness. When that happens, East and West will be monumental signposts celebrating God's diverse mercies, but not geographical or ecclesiastical barriers.

The Experience of God in the Orthodox Tradition

DANIEL J. SAHAS

No one has ever seen God. The Only-begotten Son, who is in the bosom of the Father, he has explained him" (Jn 1.18). Unspeakable, therefore, and incomprehensible is the divine. Because, "No one knows the Father, but the Son; and no one knows the Son but the Father" (Mt 11.27). The Holy Spirit also knows the things pertinent to God, just as the spirit of man knows what is in him (Cf. 1 Cor 2.11). After the primordial and blessed nature, no man has ever known God, except he to whom God revealed himself; not only no man, but not even any of the supramundane powers, I mean the Cherubim and the Seraphim.[1]

The assignment given to me for tonight is exceedingly disproportionate to my expertise and to the limitations which time and the environment impose on us. In justice, however, to Father Barringer I must confess that among three topics he proposed to me on behalf of the "St. Peter and St. Andrew Lectures," I opted, purposely, for this one; first because it was the most difficult, and second, because on a topic so existential, broad and universal as this, the lecturer hopes to find in his audience people who will sympathize with his predicament. Tonight we are all aboard the same boat—a sinking boat: the "boat" of our *reason* in the midst of the ocean of the divine. On my part I want to declare unabashedly and from the very beginning that I do not know what to say and how to say it in order to keep the "boat" afloat, be academically acceptable, provide some insights and information, and be consistent with the purpose of this lecture series, which is to foster dialogue—both spiritual and practical—between Catholics and Orthodox. From the academic point of view the subject is, perhaps, unacceptable because of its breadth, generality and possibly its pious character. Academics want things to

---

[1]John of Damascus, *Exposition of Faith* 1.I.1, ed. Bonifatius Kotter, *Die Schriften des Johannes von Damaskos* (Berlin/New York, 1973) 2, p. 7:6-13.

be scientifically precise, to have a focus and methodology—a modern intellectual heresy—and not to be of an applied spiritual concern. In this particular instance one may justifiably feel that in the midst of so much personalized, unguarded, syncretistic and misguided religiosity, the real questions about the Christian sense of the divine, let alone about the authenticity of its expressions, are either obscured or confusing. I happen to sympathize with this feeling. I would like, therefore, to propose certain limitations in the form of clarifications, in order to give focus to the subject and make it somewhat manageable.

Are we called tonight to define God? Is this possible? In the words of Maximos the Confessor, "God is known by ignorance"[2] and the only thing that we can understand of God, according to John of Damascus, is his unknowability and incomprehensibility![3] That takes care of tonight! Are we, then, to describe God from the Orthodox point of view? That might be even absurd! I am convinced with the conviction of my hope (because knowledge in this context is meaningless) that God is not Orthodox. I hope also that he is not Catholic, or Protestant, either. *Men* are Orthodox, Catholic, Protestant. The focus, therefore, of our discussion tonight is the *human* experience of God and the expression this experience takes within the Orthodox community and tradition. "Experience" is a word very much used today and, thus, much misunderstood and mistrusted. It has often become an easy escape for justifying ignorance, or for defending one's own subjective truth. Religious people, particularly, tend to speak about "experiences" and to confuse themselves and others as to what these experiences are, what are their demonstrable foundations, as well as how they are expressed. My justification in using the word is that Orthodox theology begins from a most emphatic affirmation that God is *mystery*; and the mystery is not analyzed and remains mystery. It is rather experienced and becomes more profound. The nature of theology is to be *a delving* into the divine, which to the human reason is *gnophos,* a word for "darkness" which the Greek Fathers used.[4] I will mostly be talking about expressions which reflect innermost theological experiences, drawn from, or articulated in, the biblical, patristic, liturgical, and the

---

[2]Maximos the Confessor, *Commentaries in the Book On the Divine Names,* 7.3, PG 4:352D.

[3]John of Damascus, *Exposition of Faith* 4.1.4 (Kotter, p. 13:32-33).

[4]Cf. Vladimir Lossky, *The Mystical Theology of the Eastern Church* (Cambridge/London, 1968), pp. 23-43.

practical tradition and sources.[5] *The reference to them will be, by necessity, sketchy!*

For reasons also of some kind of system and clarity, I will attempt to group these very selective expressions under three headings which, to me, are fundamental and at the same time familiar within the Christian community as a whole. I feel that Orthodox and Catholics have lost so much time already without a meaningful dialogue that there is no sense in competing for sensationalism or originality.

Transcendent and Yet Personal

The Orthodox experience of God is Trinitarian, that is *personal*. This is not a doctrine imposed from above, but a spontaneous and natural expression of the human faith in the transcendence and, at the same time, in the immanence of God. For the Orthodox, God is not a mystery for the sake of remaining unknown. He is a Being to become known, although not by means of understanding, but by means of association. The apophatic theology of the East, capsulated in the Areopagitic writings,[6] is not a negative theology, as it does not negate God. It negates (ἀπο-φάσκει) what man says *about* God; what is inferior to him, and what confines and restricts the essence of God by means of human logic or fiat, including his non-existence, or his non-relevance. For the Orthodox, God is a Being who is in relation with himself and with the world. In simple language, for the Orthodox a God who has no self-awareness cannot be God for someone else, although not everyone, or everything, that has self-awareness is God either. Relation implies a *personal* character, because πρόσωπον means turning one's face towards someone, or towards oneself.[7] God knows himself not by means of knowledge, but by his own Being. He knows himself in his own way, that is "eternally and in love," as Maximos put it.[8] The Christian faith in God is precisely a belief in a Being who *is* eternal and love. But even this "eternal" and "love" are not identical to the way we humans

---

[5] A simple but useful anthology of quotations and expressions which reflect the Orthodox ethos, or "way," has been produced by Kallistos Ware, *The Orthodox Way* (Crestwood, N.Y., 1979).

[6] Cf. especially the treatise *On the Divine Names*, PG 3:585A-996B and Maximos' *Commentaries*, PG 4:29A-416B and 416D-432C.

[7] Cf. Christos Yannaras, Τό ὀντολογικό περιεχόμενο τῆς θεολογικῆς ἐννοίας τοῦ προσώπου (Athens, 1970).

[8] Ἀχρόνως καὶ ἀγαπητικῶς, *Commentaries*, 2.3, PG 4:221A.

perceive them, because man is created, and his love is one of convention. The sense of transcendence of God and his personal Being, as well as man's inability to describe it, have been eloquently expressed through the characteristic antinomical language of the patristic literature, an example of which I want to offer now.

> Therefore, we believe in one God: one principle, without beginning, uncreated, unbegotten, indestructible and immortal, eternal, unlimited, uncircumscribed, unbounded, infinite in power, simple, uncompounded, incorporeal, unchanging, unaffected, unchangeable, inalterate, invisible, source of goodness and justice, light intellectual and inaccessible; power which no measure can give any idea of, but which is measured only by his own will, for he can do all things whatsoever he pleases; maker of all things both visible and invisible, holding together all things and conserving them, provider for all, governing and dominating and ruling over all in unending and immortal reign; without contradiction, filling all things, contained by nothing, but himself containing all things, being their conserver and first possessor; pervading all substances without being defiled, removed far beyond all things and every substance as being supersubstantial and surpassing all, supereminently divine and good and replete; appointing all the principalities and orders, set above every principality and order, above essence and life and speech and concept; light itself and goodness and being in so far as having neither being nor anything else that is from any other; the very source of being for all things that are, of life to the living, of speech to the articulate, and the cause of all good things for all; knowing all things before they begin to be; one substance, one godhead, one virtue, one will, one operation, one principality, one power, one domination, one kingdom; *known in three perfect Persons and adored with one adoration, believed in and worshiped by every rational creature, united without confusion and distinct without separation, which is beyond understanding.* We believe in Father and Son and Holy Spirit in whom we have been baptized.[9]

In this "iconic" fashion and breath-taking literary style, John of

---

[9] John of Damascus, *Exposition of Faith* 8.1.8 (Kotter, pp. 18:2-19:27). The translation is from Frederic H. Chase, *Saint John of Damascus. Writings*, The Fathers of the Church, vol. 37 (New York, 1958), pp. 176-77.

[10] In the words of Ignatios of Antioch: "Christianity is not measured by its logic, but by the degree of its own greatness;" *To the Romans* 3.3, ed. Kirsopp Lake, *The Apostolic Fathers* (London, 1965) 1, p. 228.

Damascus ridicules, I think, man's illusion that he is able to describe the mystery of God in a definite logical way.[10] On the other hand, we must remember that John of Damascus and others, although they felt so strongly about the transcendence and unknowability of God, also spoke and wrote a great deal about it; a fact which also shows the other conviction of the Christian East, that God is as close to man as man's own . . . mouth! Even more so. According to the very same statement of the Damascene, a Christian does not simply speak of God *in abstracto,* but has a knowledge of him which is an *existential experience* on account of being baptized (fully immersed) into the mystery of the Holy Trinity. Other Fathers underlined also the Orthodox assertion of the mystery of God by talking about him in terms of "silence." They were quick, however, to add that silence becomes manifest because of the Word. Thus Christ, according to Ignatios of Antioch, is ὁ λόγος ὁ ἀπὸ σιγῆς προελθών ("the Word, derived from silence").[11] The entire Palamite tradition and spirituality is nothing else but a whole way of life, distinguishing the unknowable essence of God, while experiencing, even in the body, God's own energies through the Son in the Holy Spirit—a tradition which John Meyendorff calls "a Christian Existentialism."[12]

Orthodox iconography—in itself a phenomenon of and a testimony to the antinomy of the transcendence and the immanence of the divine—when called upon to depict God, is dumbfounded and remains completely silent or "apophatic." Inside a typical Orthodox church, where every inch of wall is covered by the iconographers, one will not find any single icon of God or of the theme of the Holy Trinity. The sole iconographic theme that sometimes is identified as "The Holy Trinity" is the scene of Abraham offering hospitality to three young men who proved to be angels, and this is because the theme has traditionally been treated by Orthodox theology as a pre-figuration of the Holy Trinity.[13] A well-known example of this icon is "The Trinity" by Andrei Rublev (*ca.* 1411) now in the Tretyakov Gallery in Moscow. It is worth noticing that the inherent and foremost message of this figuration of the Trinity is of an encounter of man with the "unknown" divine, and this is in context of hospitality and eating—the most existential function and moment of man. What more can one say about the Orthodox perception of the experience of

---

[11]*To the Magnesians* 8.2 (Lake, p. 204); see also *To the Ephesians* 19.1 (Lake, p. 192).

[12]*St. Gregory Palamas and Orthodox Spirituality* (Crestwood, N.Y., 1974), pp. 119-29.

[13]Fotis Kontoglou, Ἔκφρασις τῆς ὀρθοδόξου εἰκονογραφίας (Athens, 1979), 1, p. 277. "The Holy Trinity" theme depicting the Father as an old man, the Son as a younger person seated at the right hand of the Father and the Holy Spirit as a dove flying above and between them, is of non-Orthodox origin and foreign to Orthodox sensibility.

God? As a matter of fact the entire cycle of man's experience of God is related to and articulated in the context of a meal with the divine![14]

Orthodox worship also is cognizant of the Trinitarian-personal character of God to whom it brings man in a direct and experiential way. A most characteristic example is the act and prayer of consecration of the Gifts when the Holy Trinity, itself, invisible, mystical, transcendent, is in operation:

> Again we offer Thee this real and yet bloodless sacrifice and we pray and beseech and implore Thee: Send down Thy Holy Spirit upon us and upon the gifts here set forth: And make this bread, the precious Body of Thy Christ. And what is in this cup the precious Blood of Thy Christ; changing them by Thy Holy Spirit. Amen. Amen. Amen. . . . [15]

In every private or congregational prayer also the Orthodox invokes God as the Holy Trinity:

> Most Holy Trinity, have mercy upon us.
> O Lord, pardon our sins;
> O Master, forgive our iniquities;
> O Holy One, visit and heal our infirmities,
>   For Thy Name's sake.
> Lord, have mercy. Lord, have mercy. Lord, have mercy.

Worth noticing here is the declaration of the undivided character of the Holy Trinity, with no qualifications, and immediately after the reference to man's personal relationship to God by means of a personalized adjective and supplication for each of the three Persons. One also should mention the well-known *Trisagion*, or Thrice-Holy invocation, which is on the lips of every Orthodox:

---

[14] A study of the dynamics of the meal as a place of meeting of man with God with reference to the Orthodox literature, hymnography, iconography, symbolism, and practice is still missing. The entire biblical tradition, in its most crucial and essential aspects, is unveiled in the context of a meal: for example, the Cana miracle, Jesus' visit to Zacchaeus' house, Jesus' visit to the house of Martha and Mary, the last supper, the Emmaus meal, the appearances of the resurrected Christ to his disciples, the early Christian love meals, etc.

[15] The Divine Liturgy of Saint John Chrysostom. The first sentence ("'Ἔτι προσφέρομέν σοι τὴν λογικὴν ταύτην καὶ ἀναίμακτον λατρείαν . . .'") is a trial to be translated into English.

Holy God, Holy Mighty, Holy Immortal, have mercy upon us.[16]

The practice also of the Orthodox tradition is Trinitarian. The Church as such is not perceived as a temporal, human institution, but as the divine-human reality which manifests and mirrors the life of the Holy Trinity through a community of men here on earth. It is worth noticing that in her creed, after she has declared her belief in God the Father, Son, and Holy Spirit, the Church has incorporated also her own self-awareness that reciprocates her relationship to the Holy Trinity. Thus the particular article of the Nicene-Constantinopolitan creed reads: "I believe in one, holy, catholic, and apostolic church."[17] It seems that the choice of adjectives was not accidental, but rather intentional: to make the unity of the Church correspond to the oneness of God-the-Father; her holiness, to the holiness of the Godhead revealed by the Son; and her wholeness and truthfulness, to the wholeness and truthfulness of the Spirit of God.

In a more tangible action the Orthodox proclaims his belief in the Holy Trinity, the God of personal qualities and of direct revelation to him, every time he joins his three fingers—each one of them in its own size and with its own individual fingerprints, and yet all three of one and the same hand—to make the sign of the cross.

One, of course, does not need to be reminded that every service and every prayer in the Orthodox tradition is offered "In the name of the Father, and of the Son, and of the Holy Spirit. Amen." This "Amen" at the conclusion of the invocation concludes and seals man's entire disposition and attitude towards God and his experience of him. The rest is commentary!

Finally, I would like to remind you of the fact that the Orthodox church services are notoriously long and physically exhausting, particularly because most hymns and petitions are repeated *three* times, to remind us of the Holy Trinity. If the Trinity of the Oneness of God and his Unity in Trinity is a cross to human logic, so it is to the human body as well!

As far as the character of these and many more expressions of the

---

[16]In the Greek text the phrase "have mercy upon us" is in the singular form (ἐλέησον ἡμᾶς), affirming the belief in the union of the persons in the Godhead.

[17]The adjective "apostolic" was not part of the Jerusalem creed which became the basis for this article of the Constantinopolitan creed. Its incorporation into the Nicene-Constantinopolitan creed had, probably, anti-heretical apologetic reasons; a reminder of the Apostolic tradition as a citerion of Orthodoxy. See the creed of Cyril of Jerusalem in Philip Schaff, *The Creeds of Christendom with a History and Critical Notes*, vol. 2 (rp., Grand Rapids, Mich, 1966), p. 32.

Trinitarian experience of God, they are distinctly experiential, rather than mental or logical, doxological, rather than analytical and scholastic, reflective of a personal passion and love for God. It is not coincidental that the same sources which speak so emphatically about the transcendence and the mystery of God use words such as "passion" and "eros" to describe man's motive to know God. Dionysios says that "eros" is a more divine-like word than "love,"[18] and man's motive is not simply to know, but to develop a passion for the divine (οὐ μόνον μαθὼν ἀλλὰ καὶ παθὼν τὰ θεῖα).[19]

Christocentric

The *Christian* experience of God is, by definition, Christocentric.[20] Going around in circles certainly leads us nowhere, but what about if we are already there![21] A mental separation of theology from Christology is, for a Christian, a schizophrenic religious exercise and experience, as it abides in a god of the philosophers while flirting with the God of revelation.[22] Even modern humanists, not theologians, who have been influenced by the Orthodox environment, discern that truth in Orthodox Christianity is not something, but *someone*: God-made-man, thus a *perfect* man.[23] For the faithful this *perfect* man is God incarnate, thus *perfect* God as well. How else could God—in the way we spoke of him before—reveal himself to man, that is, "face" man directly, if he would not himself become man? As simple and naive as this logic is, so God-like it is as an action of a personal God. Paul called it *kenosis*, that

---

[18]"Ἔδοξέ τισι τῶν καθ' ἡμᾶς ἱερολόγων καὶ θειότερον εἶναι τὸ τοῦ ἔρωτος ὄνομα τοῦ τῆς ἀγάπης." *On the Divine Names* 4.12, PG 3:709A-B.

[19]*On the Divine Names* 2.9, PG 3:648B.

[20]Cf. also Georges Florovsky, "Patristic Theology and the Ethos of the Orthodox Church," in his *Collected Works*, vol. 4: *Aspects of Church History* (Belmont, Mass., 1975), p. 24.

[21]I have borrowed this characteristic phrase from the film "Islamic Mysticism. The Sufi Way," written by Huston Smith. I find the phrase particularly applicable to describe the place of Christ in the Christian tradition, especially in Orthodoxy, with reference to man's experience of God. Sufism gives this place to human emotion and feeling. In the Maulawiya (Mavlevi) movement which the film describes, the whirling dervishes dance around themselves, in a circumference, the center of which is occupied by the whirling sufi master—which shows that Sufism is, ultimately, an anthropocentric experience.

[22]As Jaroslav Pelikan has put it, interpreting the Greek Fathers, theology is not a science of divine ontology, but of divine revelation; *The Spirit of Eastern Christendom (600-1700)* (Chicago, 1974), p. 33.

[23]K. I. Dedopoulos, Οἱ ἄνθρωποι καὶ τὰ ὁράματα, (Athens, 1962), p. 49.

is, "emptiness" (Phil 2.8). Orthodox hymnology called it "a strange and odd mystery" with which man is faced.[24] Thus, whereas a moment ago we were talking about the ineffable glory of God, now we are speaking about the inexplicable "emptiness" of God, an emptiness which does not diminish the mystery of God, but brings it down to the level of man. The Christian understanding of God's revelation is the very event of the incarnation of the Logos in Christ. That is why the Orthodox, using the same gesture and the same hand with which he proclaims his faith in the Holy Trinity, proclaims also his faith in Christ who is "one of the Holy Trinity" (εἷς ὢν τῆς Ἁγίας Τριάδος).

The Christocentric revelation of the mystery of God has immense consequences for man, consequences which the Orthodox tradition has only underlined. First and foremost, it defines man's knowledge of God in terms of *actual* association with (indeed, incorporation in) Christ. In the earliest Christian community, "Christian" meant not simply the believer in, or the follower of Christ, but the imitator of Christ,[25] with two very tangible and dramatic manifestations: martyrdom and monasticism. Secondly, it redefines man not as a "fallen"[26] humanity, but in terms of man's ontological being and value, for which God assumed human nature παρὰ φύσιν (not being himself of that nature), in order for man to become God by grace.[27] Thus baptism for the Orthodox is not simply an act of religious initiation. It is the event of the rebirth of a person into "a new man" (Col 3.10), an event which is accentuated in the Orthodox tradition by giving to the child for the first time his or her name—a *Christian* name. Baptism is sharing in the death and the resurrection of Christ (Rom 6.3-4), dramatized by the complete immersion into the water. The "new man" is now Χριστοφόρος (Christ-bearing) because, as the Orthodox Church sings: "Those of you who have been baptized in Christ, you have put onto yourselves Christ himself."[28] But the baptism in Christ is a baptism "In the name of the Father, and of the Son, and of the Holy Spirit," that is, an entrance into the mystery of the Holy

---

[24]"Μυστήριον ξένον ὁρῶ καὶ παράδοξον." Irmos, Ninth Ode of Christmas Katavasiai.

[25]Ignatios of Antioch, *To the Magnesians* 4.1 (Lake, p. 200); *To the Romans* 2.1; 3.2 (Lake, pp. 226, 228); *To the Smyrnaians* 4.2; 11.1 (Lake, pp. 256, 262/264); *To Saint Polycarp* 7.3 (Lake, pp. 274/276).

[26]This common expression has connotations of a personal relationship with, or "vision" of God which points obviously to the experiential character of man's knowledge of God.

[27]Cf. Lossky, *The Mystical Theology*, pp. 114-34.

[28]"Ὅσοι εἰς Χριστὸν ἐβαπτίσθητε, Χριστὸν ἐνεδύσασθε. Ἀλληλούϊα."

Trinity. That is why the newly-baptized one is called "newly illuminated" (νεοφώτιστος). He is θεοφόρος (God-bearing).[29]

To enumerate the ways in which the Orthodox tradition expresses its Christocentric experience of God would require a lecture of its own. Let me mention briefly only a few.

1. *The Icon*

While no icon of God has been attempted, the icon of Christ predominates inside an Orthodox church or home.

On account of the incarnation Christ is, truly, one of us. Thus, what the biblical narrative has transmitted to us in words, the icon narrates[30] for us in color. The icon in the Orthodox tradition is something essentially different from a religious painting or picture. It is a liturgical act and a "theology in color."[31] As a matter of fact, the only justification that the Orthodox tradition has to offer in order to explain how it is that Christ can be depicted, is the reality of the incarnation itself.[32] Thus the adoration offered to the icon is an adoration of honor to the person depicted on it, because "the honor to the icon is transferred to the prototype," to use the classical statement of Saint Basil,[33] and the worship offered to Christ is a worship offered to the Holy Trinity because Christ "is one of the Holy Trinity, *glorified together with the Father and with the Holy Spirit.*"[34]

2. *The Liturgical Experience*

In the Orthodox tradition the liturgy is a celebration of the mystery of the incarnation and a *re-enactment* of the very life of Christ on earth. Even if there had been no other means of expressing and living the experience of God than the liturgy, the Orthodox would have been

---

[29]Cf. Ignatios of Antioch, *To the Ephesians* 9.2 (Lake, p. 182).

[30]One of the most common names for icons has been "narrative" (ἱστόρησις), or "story" (ἱστορία), or hagiography (painting of holy things). Kontoglou, Ἔκφρασις, 1, p. 416.

[31]Cf. Eugene N. Trubetskoi, *Icons: Theology in Color* (Crestwood, N.Y., 1973).

[32]Cf. the Sixth *Act* of the Seventh Ecumenical Synod in G. D. Mansi, *Sacrorum Conciliorum Nova et Amplissima Collectio*, (Florence, 1767) 13, pp. 204A-364D.

[33]*On the Holy Spirit* 18.45, PG 32:149C.

[34]The Divine Liturgy of Saint John Chrysostom.

satisfied with that alone. As a matter of fact where and when everything else is impossible or has failed, Orthodox worship has proven a most effective way to bring man face to face with God. Orthodoxy in Russia and elsewhere is a case in point. The experience in the liturgy is one of participation in and a foretaste of the Kingdom here and now, a sense of incorruptibility and otherworldliness, and yet from now and within this very world. The Divine Liturgy of Saint John Chrysostom actually begins with the words: "Blessed is the Kingdom of the Father, and of the Son, and of the Holy Spirit, now and ever and unto ages of ages. Amen."

3. *The Sacramental Experience*

What the West calls "sacraments" the East calls "mysteries," as these are sanctifying acts and experiences of God who is, above all, mystery. Thus, although the Orthodox Church maintains seven sacraments, she is not eager either to defend or to rationalize the number, for the grace of God who is One is a mystery as well. Man is able to participate in the mystery of God existentially, through Christ, precisely because in Christ "the whole fullness of deity dwells bodily" (Col 2.9). Thus in baptism, as we said, man becomes himself *Christophoros* (Christ-bearing), and he is introduced into the mystery of the Holy Trinity. In Chrismation he becomes *Christos*, not by nature, but by grace, anointed with the gifts of the Holy Spirit whose advent became manifest because of the incarnation of the Logos. In *metanoia* (rather than "confession") what is sacramental is man's coming to his senses and distinguishing what is not God-like, thus "changing of his mind." This is possible because Christ assumed to himself the fallen nature and provided for it a prototype. In Communion man is invited to a mystical paschal meal, where the Lamb of God offers himself as "medicine of immortality, an antidote against death," to quote Ignatios of Antioch.[35] In marriage the relationship of two persons becomes, indeed, a divine union in the pattern of the union of the Holy Trinity and of the two natures in the one person of Christ: "without confusion, without change, without division, without separation," to use the wording of the Christological Definition of Chalcedon (451). In Ordination man is called to continue the priestly function of Christ himself and thus make the union of the "bride" with him always contemporary and always existential. In holy unction man

---

[35] *To the Ephesians* 20.2 (Lake, p. 194).

is able to ask for and acquire the healing experience of the grace of God, because Christ himself felt and healed pain.

4. *The Experience of the Church*

But where the Orthodox tradition has something even more specific to say is in the context of the reality of the Church, a central issue for use in the ecumenical dialogue. There is no dichotomy or separation between Christ and the Church in the Orthodox tradition, because there can be no Christ *in abstracto*. The Church as a divine-human reality exists, because of Christ. Christ is never alone. He is always the head of his Body. "The Body of Christ is not an appendix," wrote Georges Florovsky.[36] It is rather absurd to talk about the Church as if she existed in the stratosphere, and at the same time believe in the *incarnation* of the Logos. As it is equally absurd to speak of the Church as simply a community of believers, and at the same time believe that Christ is *God* incarnate: the relationship of the visible community to Christ is not one of acquaintance but of association, one of identification with the "flesh" of Christ in space and time. The Church is the derivative of the incarnation, not its inventor.

5. *Personal Practice and Spirituality*

The Orthodox is not afraid of making Christ familiar to him for fear of humiliating his being. Christ did so himself by becoming man. Man cannot make him any less than he is. Thus Christ is part of an Orthodox home and part of the family. His name is invoked in prayer, adoration, and supplication many times a day. Men and women are called by his name and sign their name by his name. The entire cycle of "the year of the holiness of the Lord" (this is the traditional name for the ecclesiastical year) is Christocentric. The mystic, the monk, the pious—more in the past but also in the present—repeat ceaselessly his name in the prayer of the heart or the prayer of Jesus ("Jesus Christ Son of God, have mercy on me a sinner": an Orthodox *dhikr*) as a means of keeping the mind concentrated on God and purified from pride.[37] Even simple and unsophisticated people have developed a personal familiarity with Jesus. In the church of the Monastery of the Holy Trinity in Meteora

---

[36]"Patristic Theology," p. 25.

[37]Cf., for example, the story of popular spirituality narrated in *The Way of a Pilgrim*, trans. R. M. French (New York, 1952).

(central Greece) one finds on the left hand side, facing the iconostasis, the icon of the Holy Trinity in its traditional symbolic figuration of the hospitality of the three angels, and on the right hand side the icon of Christ wearing the seventeenth-century local costume of a Karagouni.[38] Those who are familiar with the particular order of the icons on the iconostasis will be able to appreciate the meaning of this contrast ... The Orthodox even "touches" and works with the elements which become the instruments or the actualities of Christ's physical presence in the world. Like the iconographer, a woman kneads bread as man's offering to God (*prosphoron*). But in doing so (working the yeast, the flour, the water and the other ingredients) and by making two loaves of bread which she places one on top of the other forming one loaf, she proclaims in action her faith in, and her experience of God, incarnate in Christ. The seal of the bread brings together the whole of existence, divine and human: the Lamb, the all-holy Mother, the angels, the saints, martyrs, the church of the past and the church of the present. It is from that same bread which she made that she and the congregation will partake in the Body of Christ. The same is true with the man who prepared the wine. Man is called to the mystical supper with the food that he himself prepared. He is not a passive attendant; he is an active participant and a co-worker (συνεργός) with the divine. It is interesting that the most solemn moment in the Orthodox liturgy is when *we* offer to God what is *his* so that he may make them for us the precious Body of his Christ and precious Blood of his Christ.[39] This, obviously, is not an intellectual, emotional, symbolic acquaintance; it is a physical, existential, wholesome union with the divine. It is after their transformation that what has been elevated from the common to the holy is now returned to the holy ones.[40] There can be no better recycling and conservation, than by offering the material to God to make it holy.

If one wants to qualify with one word the character of the Christocentric experience of God he can describe it with one word only, Christological: fully cognizant of the mystery of the divine and of the realism of the human in the one person of Christ. This is what makes the Orthodox experience of God through Christ so personal and physical and at the same time so "iconic" and symbolic. Christ in the Orthodox Church is the sole cause of man's *experiential* knowledge of God. The apophatic

---

[38]Sister Theotekni, *Meteora. The Rocky Forest of Greece* (Athens, 1977), p. 97.

[39]"Thine of what is Thine (Τὰ Σὰ ἐκ τῶν Σῶν ...)": The Divine Liturgy of Saint John Chrysostom.

[40]"Τὰ ἅγια, τοῖς ἁγίοις," ibid.

theology of the East never developed into an independent and autonomous expression of God's experience; thus it never became a negative theology. It remained always positive, precisely on account of Christology. Its attraction has remained fresh through the ages, especially in moments of resurgence of rationalism, because in its essence it is Christocentric and points to Christ directly. On the day of the feast of Saint Andrew it is worth remembering a minor incident in his life, from the very few that have been transmitted to us. When some Hellenized Jews came to Jerusalem and asked Philip to show them Jesus, Philip went to Andrew. Now, fortunately, Andrew did not take them to his brother Peter, nor did he give them a lecture on Jesus, but rather he took them to Jesus directly (Jn 12.22). I find this incident prophetic and meaningful.

Existential and Whole

In the Orthodox tradition man has a special affinity with and reverence for nature and the material creation. The Orthodox sees no dichotomy, particularly no moral or ethical one, between matter and spirit. Matter is not by nature evil, nor spirit by nature good. This is an unwarranted oversimplification. Thus, God in the Orthodox tradition is experienced wholly and existentially in and through the material creation. The mysteries, or the sacraments, that we talked about before are the most eloquent manifestations of this whole experience.

Matter, externals, things, play such an important role that without them there can be no sacrament. It is not enough to say that an Orthodox experiences God through, let us say, worship; the opposite is also true. The whole man and the entire creation are called together and become part of worship, something which *in itself* is an experience of God as cause, creator and redeemer of the entire creation. In that sense the Orthodox Church shares through material things and goods her conviction that the grace of God is transmitted, or that the sense of the divine becomes manifest to man through all means, visible and invisible. A seven-year-old friend of my son, who is not Orthodox and whom we have invited a few times to come to our church, once observed and related this to my son: "Every time I come to your church they always give me something. They do not do that in our church." At one time he happened to be with us at the Vesper service of Easter Sunday when at the end the priest distributed to the people red eggs. At another time you get a flower. On the day of the Elevation of the Cross you receive a sprig of basil; on Palm Sunday a palm leaf; on Epiphany, blessed water to bless your house; at a thanksgiving service (*Artoklasia*) a piece of bread, and on every Sunday and holiday, or any day of the week when the liturgy is celebrated, everyone who has not taken communion, is "sent out in peace" with a piece of bread as *antidoron*, instead of the Gift. Everyone is invited to the paschal meal, and although each one chooses for himself a different "garment" and a different way of partaking, the Church proclaims in the words of John Chrysostom:

> Rich and poor, dance with one another . . .
> The table is full; all of you fare sumptuously.
> The calf is plenty; let no one go forth hungry.[41]

With such reverence for the material creation, the Orthodox Church prays not only for the salvation of our souls but also for the welfare of things and animals. In every service there are repeated petitions "for this city and for every city and land and for the faithful who dwell in them"; "for seasonable weather, for the abundance of the fruits of the earth and for peaceful times"; "for the president, or the king, or the queen, or the head of State of the land"; "for the clergy and the laity"; "for those who travel by land, by water, and (now) by air." In the Orthodox prayer book there are even special prayers "for laying the foundation of a new home," "for entering a new home," "for farms, gardens and vineyards," "for the blessing of the seeds," "blessing the threshing," "for the blessing of the wine," "blessing of a flock" and "for sick animals!" In all these circumstances the occasion becomes the means of recalling an equivalent event in Christ's life, thus making the occasion a Christocentric encounter with the divine.[42] The Orthodox tradition treats these

---

[41] From the Catechetical Sermon of Saint John Chrysostom read on Easter Sunday. I do not know which one has influenced which—the cultural peculiarity or the religious experience. But hospitality is a trade mark of Orthodox countries, families, and individuals. No matter how poor or destitute an Orthodox is, he feels it an obligation to offer something edible to a guest. My students in both travel seminars in 1978 and 1980 remarked that we were nowhere in an Orthodox environment when we were not offered a sweet and a glass of water. The hospitality of Abraham and his encounter with the divine in that context, together with the biblical admonition in Hebrews 13.2, have certainly fashioned or strengthened a practice in the Orthodox Church and in the Orthodox culture.

[42] Thus, for example, on entering a new home the prayer recalls Jesus entering the house of Zacchaeus. On blessing the wine the prayer recalls the miracle at Cana. On praying for sick animals, the prayer recalls that God is the creator and the sovereign of all creation which He has entrusted to man for his use and service.

events not as incidents of the past but as contemporary events within a continuous and uninterrupted "today," since the divine is beyond time. Thus it is "today" that "Christ is born..." (Christmas service); "Today the nature of the waters is sanctified..." (Epiphany Day); "Today He is hanged on a tree, He who fixed the earth on the waters..." (Holy Friday); "Today Hades cries out groaning..." (Holy Saturday); "Today Christ is risen..." (Easter Sunday). And on today's feast of Saint Andrew the Church sings:

> Now Bethsaida may rejoice
> for in thee, as from a mystical pot
> flowered forth most sweet-smelling lilies,
> Peter and Andrew...[43]

The Orthodox Church even has a special service in which she blesses the water, and through it the entire creation. Interestingly enough, the day chosen for this blessing is the day of Jesus' baptism, the day on which the divine enters bodily into the material creation, and man and the creation are presented with the epiphany of the Holy Trinity![44] This is a revolutionary perception of the experience of God that Orthodox tradition suggests through this service. God is not somewhere far and high. His presence is as close as the creation which you and I touch and depend upon: the water we drink, the water we cook with, the water we swim in, the water we use to water our fields and plants, the water of the seas we travel, of the lakes and of the rivers we enjoy, the water which, frozen, we skate on. In the Orthodox tradition man does not need to go far in order to experience God. God does not sanctify man without sanctifying also the nature within which man lives. That is why in the same service of Epiphany the Orthodox sings:

> Sanctify me and the water, O Savior,
> You who have lifted up the sin of the world.[45]

It would be absurd to assume that God saved man and left the creation corrupted. If the thirsty desert is now delighted and springs forth crocuses, as the Epiphany reading from Isaiah says,[46] then man, too, has

---

[43] Menologion for November 30: Sticheron Prosomoion of the First Tone.

[44] "... ἡ τῆς Τριάδος ἐφανερώθη προσκύνησις ...": Troparion of Epiphany Day.

[45] Doxastikon of the First Hour of Epiphany.

[46] Isaiah 35.1-10 is the reading of the First Hour of Epiphany.

something to be looking forward to and something that reminds him of his salvation. From its crudest to its most purified form nature is enwrapped by the numinous and as such it is used in the Orthodox tradition as a "liturgical" means.

Thus, even the word itself is perceived as material, as food not of the mind or of the soul but of the body as well. The word of God is to be heard, to be sung, to be touched, to be handled, to be seen, even to be kissed. The gospel in the Orthodox tradition is not the Word of God. Christ himself is the Word of God, incarnate. Thus the gospel as the record *about* the incarnate Word is read, and preached, but also laboriously decorated and ornamented, taken out in a procession accompanied by lights, touched with reverence and awe, kissed and venerated. Not only man with all his senses experiences the word of God, but also the entire material creation, in its own manifold ways, participates in the experience and in the proclamation of the Word.

The Christian East also called and treated formulations of faith not as doctrines but as "borders" (*horoi*) of faith within which the whole of human existence, and not only the mind, behaves and expresses itself. Again, the icon, made of simple material substances, is not an aesthetic art in the Orthodox tradition, but an *horos* of faith—that is, an expression of the Christological faith—and a liturgical act which man uses to relate to the prototype.

The Orthodox disposition towards the material creation, or life and culture in general, is one of integration rather than of exclusion. The Orthodox experience of God is a matter of a whole way of life, rather than of a compartmentalized bahavior. Orthodox monasticism is, perhaps, one of the most characteristic examples of the integration of many forms and expressions into a self-contained way of life. But it is not the norm of the Orthodox tradition; it is the daring choice for the few, although it has affected all. Orthodox monasticism is ascetic, contemplative, aesthetic, apophatic, Christocentric, practical, doxological—all of these come together into *one* order. It is a martyrdom (μαρτύριον) and a witness (μαρτυρία), which are two sides of the same coin. The monk has made the experience of God his concentrated "business." Whether he has succeeded or not is immaterial for us to discuss. The Orthodox tradition—and far beyond that—has definitely been affected by those who have succeeded; and most of these have remained unknown.

Byzantine society attempted to transform the entire social fabric and life into a structured experience of the divine, in a kind of *Civitas Dei* on earth, something which, from the Orthodox point of view, the Catholic West has not yet overcome. The Byzantine experience is a story both of success and of failure, and the Orthodox tradition has profited immensely from both. If nothing else, the whole "experiment" has shown that such a society *is* a possibility, but not a reality of this world. It furthermore underlined the fact that an experience of God is not a matter of mass-feeling and behavior—which is a contradiction in terms—but rather a matter of a profound sensitivity towards the divine and of a personal quest for the Kingdom within. On the other hand what have shown great resilience with respect to time and to the nature of this world as a community or body structure, are monasticism and most definitely the parish life, as the microcosm and the "little leaven" (1 Cor 5.6)—something to which the Protestant West has not yet given a thoughtful chance.

The Soteriological Character of the Orthodox Experience

We defined the experience of God in the Orthodox tradition as transcendent and yet personal, Christocentric, existential and all-inclusive. Although the examples of expressions I have given speak for themselves, I feel that one might still leave from here with the impression that *experience* as such—even if this is a profound wholesome involvement and not a psychological illusion or delusion—is the motivation for an Orthodox to seek God. After all, the prevalent impression among most non—Orthodox is that the Orthodox tradition is mystically inclined, liturgically oriented, hierarchically structured, expressive in its life, etc. All these terms may say something about the manifestations, but they say very little about the essential driving force of the Orthodox tradition.

I cannot but be brief and definite in bringing this lecture to its close. The Orthodox has no interest in the experience of God either for the sake of experience, or for reasons of having a mystical exaltation, or for training his mind with spiritual and metaphysical questions, or for reasons of justifying his way of life or his adherence to a certain religious group. I would put it bluntly that, from the vantage point of the essence of Orthodoxy, man's interest in the experience of God is because of his yearning for salvation. As a matter of fact this is, I believe, the sole *raison d'être* of Christianity to begin with. Christianity is a religious experience of redemptive revelation, a revelation which, in itself, is a redemptive experience.

Having spoken at some length about the unknowability and incomprehensibility of God—and the Orthodox tradition is a product and a reflection of this theological posture—and at the same time having spoken of the manifold material sources and expressions of the Orthodox life and spirituality, one might be left wondering how the two go together. Of course one has to remember that in order to see the light one has to strike the match. The light is neither restricted, nor exhausted by any one match, not even by all the matches put together. The light of the match does not proclaim the limitation of light, but rather the limitation of the match itself. The spark is the glimpse of light and, although not the light in its ultimate being and in its absolute simplicity, it is *light* in its ontology and wholeness. As long as one keeps these analogies in mind, he attributes no insult to the light by striking the match! Unless he prefers to maintain the "dignity" of the light by *not* striking the match. Even then, light will ontologically exist, but man himself will be in darkness, if at all, in life . . .

Catholic-Orthodox Dialogue: The Present Position

ROBERT BARRINGER C. S. B.

We have come to a point in the Ecumenical Movement where quick progress has been replaced by hard slogging, where discouragement is easy, and where many are tempted by the roughness of the landscape to "pack it all in" and return to the more familiar and comforting perspectives of their own traditions: those four walls and that old, overstuffed furniture we seem to know so well. I hope, though, that the situation of those of us who are here tonight is more like that of the first disciples who followed Jesus, who left everything behind in a decisive way and who, when it got to the hard part, the point where others "drew back and went about with Him no more" (Jn 6.66), found that they had burned their bridges and that their lot was cast, once and for all, with His: "Lord, to whom shall we go? You have the words of eternal life" (Jn 6.68).

The unity of the Church is either some rhetorical flourish or harebrained scheme of our own devising, or else it is the will of God and the call of God and we should not be surprised if it *costs* us to pursue it. The cost is real and perseverance is everything, but we should also have enough of a sense of humor to recognize that wry note in the voice of the author of Hebrews who reminds us that in spite of all our struggles and difficulties in this matter, "we have not yet carried our resistance to the point of shedding our blood" (Heb 12.4). I will come back to this theme of patience and perseverance at the end of the Lecture.

The title of this evening's Lecture is "Catholic-Orthodox Dialogue: The Present Position," and under that umbrella I will try to do three things. The first will be to give you the outlines of the present state of the ecumenical dialogue between the Eastern Orthodox and the Roman Catholic churches, and especially with regard to the highest level of that dialogue: what has been happening; what is likely to happen; what problems have been encountered. The second thing I would like to do is to present some reflections on the first document produced by the Joint International Commission for Theological Dialogue between the two traditions. The third and final part of the lecture will attempt to relate what has been seen in the first two sections to the local situation in Canada, and even here in Toronto. As we will see, the document from the Commission speaks a great deal of the "local nature" of the Church, and thus encourages and even demands that we reflect together on the real circumstances and the real contributions that can be made by Christians in our own time and place.

Church historians—of which I am one—are used to seeing "currents," "trends" and developments in church life which may take centuries to unfold or bear fruit. It is easy to be glib about the clarity of such trends, especially with hindsight. It is much harder to know what it felt like *from inside* in the middle of such a "trend" (as, for example, the Reform currents of the fourteenth-sixteenth centuries or the estrangement of Christian East and West during the fifth-ninth centuries) when there were no maps and charts from church historians to tell people where they were. Anyone concerned with the work of ecumenism today is very probably in the same kind of position. We are disposed by our TV culture to look for solutions to our problems in neat half-hour or hour-long packages; this is not likely to be the best preparation to understand what is before all else a work of faith.

The Present State of Ecumenical Dialogue

The first document from the Joint International Commission was published in July of 1982. It will be helpful, however, to put this document in the context of Orthodox-Roman Catholic relations during the last twenty years. I say twenty years advisably because the document is the first major statement which both the Orthodox and Roman Catholic churches have drawn up in common since the declaration issued by the Greek and Latin Christians gathered at the Council of Florence in 1439. The history of Orthodox-Roman Catholic relations between that time and our own is a many-sided one, and often makes for sad reading. In general it has been marked by suspicion, mutual ignorance and a fair degree of open hostility.

In our own century the stage was set for a change of mood by the impact of the liturgical and ecumenical movements and by the renewal of interest in the writings of the Fathers of the Church. This latter element in particular has made it possible for Orthodox and Roman Catholics to rediscover how much they actually share in common and to realize how deep a foundation the tradition of the Undivided Church provides for their future relations.

The initiative for change was born in the two most significant events of the previous generation for Orthodox and Catholics: the convoking of the Second Vatican Council (1962-1965) on the Roman Catholic side, and on the Orthodox side the holding of a series of *Pan-Orthodox* Conferences (1961ff.) which have enabled the numerous autonomous national Orthodox churches to deepen in a practical way their own sense of *being* the Church universal and to explore their relationship *as Church* with other Christian groups. At a very early stage (1963/4) both the Vatican Council and the Pan-Orthodox Conferences expressed the desire to seek restoration of full communion between them by means of a dialogue conducted on the basis of equality.

What has happened since that wish was first expressed in 1963/4 is a rather complicated business. Let me try to lay out the elements for you now. It will help in the interpretation of our document.

The first element to be taken into account is what might be called the "inner life" of the two churches. For Roman Catholics this inner life has been dominated of course by the Second Vatican Council and its implementation in the life of the Roman Catholic Church since 1965. We are still too close to these events and their attendant struggles and reflections to be able to make any sure identification of their underlying pattern and significance. What is certainly of great importance is the brute fact that so much which was characteristic of "Latin" Christianity over the centuries has now changed. This has been most obvious in the area of liturgy, but it is true also in the field of theological method and the wider customs of church life. This change has proved a bit unsettling to many Orthodox observers. Sometimes Orthodox reaction has been positive; often it has been negative—even when the older model of Latin practice and custom was itself disliked by Eastern Christians: there is often something regrettable in losing "the devil you know."

The inner life of the Orthodox Church in the last generation has been held up to less public scrutiny than has been true for Catholics. Four Pan-Orthodox Conferences were held between the years 1961 and 1968 and these have led to the project of convoking a General Synod of the entire Eastern Orthodox Church: in effect, an Eighth Ecumenical Synod. This project is still unknown to most Western Christians, including Roman Catholics, but is being pursued in various ways. A permanent Secretariat has been set up at Chambésy in Switzerland and two Pre-Conciliar Conferences have been held there in 1976 and 1982.

The Conference in 1976 established an agenda for the future General Synod/Ecumenical Synod which included the following themes: marriage legislation; revision of the calendar (especially touching the question of a common date for Easter); legislation regarding fasting; the problems created by the presence of Orthodox churches outside traditional Orthodox lands and established jurisdictions (the problem of the "diaspora"); relations of the Orthodox Church with the rest of the Christian world and with the Ecumenical Movement as such; the relation of the Church to the context and problems of the modern world. The second Pre-Conciliar Conference (1982) discussed the first three of these topics: marriage, the calendar and fasting. Questions related to mixed marriages did not seem to pose any great problems at the Conference, and the normal expectation that children of mixed marriages should be raised as Orthodox remained as it was. The idea that widowed clergy (deacons and priests) might be allowed to remarry was rejected because of the resistance to this that was anticipated among the people. With respect to calendar matters, a common date for Easter was declared to be desirable, but note was taken of serious divisions existing among Orthodox and the necessity to prepare the people as a whole beforehand if any changes were to have a chance of acceptance. In the area of fasting, more study was also recommended and the topic was left over for the next Conference whose agenda would also include: relations of the Orthodox Church with the rest of the Christian world, with the Ecumenical Movement and with the modern world. The whole matter of the "diaspora," which is perhaps the most difficult of all the issues on the agenda, has been postponed to a rather distant future.

It may be true that Orthodox and Roman Catholics are influenced in some slight ways by this "inner" agenda within each church, but it is clear that the ordinary Catholic and the ordinary Orthodox is much more concerned with what is happening *inside* his own community than he is with the matter of relations *between* the two churches. Ecumenism remains an "extra."

The second element to be taken into account in dealing with the last twenty years is the fact that both the Roman Catholic Church and the Eastern Orthodox Church are engaged in bi-lateral ecumenical dialogue and discussions with other Christian traditions: Anglican, Lutheran, Reformed, Baptist and others. A certain overlapping of themes and participants in these dialogues can be helpful but the differing time-tables of the various discussions can be a problem. The theme of the Papacy, for example, has been dealt with already in bi-lateral Lutheran/Roman Catholic and Anglican/Roman Catholic dialogues, but it has been deliberately been kept out of the discussion which has so far taken place between Orthodox and Roman Catholics. Can Roman Catholics begin discussing this topic with Orthodox Christians and not feel "bound" by what has been said already and agreed upon in the other dialogues? Orthodox are in the same position in their own bi-lateral dialogues with the Oriental Orthodox churches and with the Anglican communion. The Anglican willingness to allow the *Filioque* to be dropped from the Creed must inevitably be part of what Orthodox carry over into their dialogue with the Roman Catholic Church.

It is hard to tell how significant is this fragmentation of ecumenical involvement and activity for both churches. It will certainly be a little distracting and the temptation must exist (at least unconsciously) to have certain priorities which may prove hurtful to others. Orthodox/Roman Catholic dialogue has something of the flavor of a main event for the churches involved, and if the other bi-lateral dialogues are put into the background or "on hold," there will be a natural enough resentment on the part of many of the Protestant communities who have been bearing the heat of the ecumenical day from the beginning.

The third and final element to be taken into account when looking back over the last twenty years is the shape of bi-lateral Orthodox/Roman Catholic relations. These have taken, rather self-consciously, a double form for which the terms "dialogue of love" and "dialogue of truth" have been coined.

In response to the suspicion felt by many Orthodox towards the Roman Catholic Church, it was decided that immediate official theological discussions between the two churches would prove premature and fruitless. It was crucial, therefore, to build up first of all a network of personal contacts and to lay the foundations of deeper mutual understanding between the churches so that—when it came—official theological discussion might have some hope for success. The unforgettable image of this dialogue of love was the picture of Pope Paul VI and Patriarch Athenagoras I embracing in the Holy Land in January of 1964. The underlying sense of this dialogue was set forth by the same two leaders in a joint statement issued after Patriarch Athenagoras' visit to Rome in 1967:

> They acknowledge that a true dialogue of charity, which should be the foundation of all relationships among them and among their Churches, has to be rooted in total loyalty to the unique Lord Jesus Christ, and in mutual respect for each other's traditions. Any element strengthening the bonds of charity, communion, and common action is a cause of spiritual rejoicing, and has to be promoted; whatever might prejudice this charity, communion, and common acting, is to be eliminated with the grace of God and with the power of the Holy Spirit. Pope Paul VI and the Ecumenical Patriarch Athenagoras I

believe that the dialogue of charity between their churches will bear the fruits of unselfish collaboration at the level of common action in the pastoral, social, and intellectual field, in reciprocal respect for each other's loyalty to his own church. They look forward to establishing regular and deep contacts between Catholic and Orthodox pastors for the benefit of the faithful.[1]

It is very important to realize that this "dialogue of love" must be pursued not only between pope and patriarch (Rome and Constantinople), but between the Roman Catholic Church and each of the autocephalous communities that make up the Orthodox Church. If, in 1964, pope and patriarch were more or less isolated figures, they now represent the tip of an iceberg: the main body of the iceberg consists of countless personal contacts and individual acts of reciprocal collaboration between Roman Catholics and Orthodox all around the world. The extent of these contacts should not be exaggerated, but the results of this first dialogue have been real and substantial enough that by 1975 the moment had come to begin preparations for that other dialogue, the dialogue of truth.[2]

This second dialogue tends to attract all the attention because of its historical and international character, but this focusing of attention would be an unfortunate thing if it discouraged discussion and dialogue at a more local level. The fruitful meetings of Orthodox and Roman Catholics in the United States provide an excellent example of something valuable and real which cannot be replaced by what happens "higher up."

A quick look at the events to date in the theological dialogue will be worthwhile. On November 30, 1979, during the visit of Pope Paul II to the Church of the Ecumenical Patriarch Demetrios at the Phanar, the announcement was made that an International Commission was to be established to pursue theological dialogue between Orthodox and Roman Catholics. The first meeting of the Commission took place at Patmos and Rhodes in May and June of 1980. Sixty participants were involved and the agenda, structure and principles of the dialogue were planned and discussed. The most important of these principles was to move from what is *common* to both traditions rather than to focus on what separates the two sides. This seemed to all a more promising way to achieve positive results in areas of dispute. The first theme chosen for reflection and

---

[1] Cited in Eleuterio F. Fortino, "The Catholic-Orthodox Dialogue," *One in Christ*, 18 (1982) 194-203 at pp. 197-98.

[2] The two dialogues must of course run concurrently. It would be absurd to think of them as elements of a relay race, with love "dropping out" as truth takes over.

discussion was that of the sacraments or "mysteries" in general, and, more specifically, "The Mystery of the Church and the Eucharist in the Light of the Mystery of the Holy Trinity."[3]

From June of 1980 to May of 1981 three subcommissions met and their work was subsequently brought together by a coordinating committee. The second plenary session of the International Theological Commission took place at Munich from June 30 to July 6, 1982 and it was this meeting that led to the revision and publication of the document we will be examining. The document was published with a view to informing the members of the two churches about the work of the Commission and to solicit views and reactions from the churches as a whole. The date and place of the next meeting of the Commission have not yet been set but the topic for the next meeting has been chosen: Faith, Sacraments and Unity. Particular questions regarding the sacraments of initiation will be dealt with, and it is hard to see how the question of inter-communion can be avoided, given the nature of the theme chosen.

Two further brief observations before we turn to the document itself. There are many signs that a greater sense of trust and fellowship has grown up since the 1980 meeting. Pope Paul II remarked to members of the delegation on the feast of Saint Andrew how much more satisfying it was to speak with people who were present than it was to be restricted to communication by letter. The value of these growing personal relationships will certainly make itself felt. On the other hand, the absence from both delegations of the most significant theologians of the age may be a real weakness in the long run. Age, sickness and death have combined to keep the "big names" of this century off the list of those who make up the delegations; this is on both sides. Whether this will mean that the dialogue will not be representa-

---

[3] The difficulties attached to the opening session of the Joint Theological Commission are well known, but one underlying principle perhaps deserves to be mentioned. Shortly before the session was to meet, the Vatican announced the appointment of certain Eastern Catholic bishops to sensitive areas (Athens, Roumania) and also established diplomatic relations with the government of Greece. These actions were interpreted as provocative (especially within the Church of Greece delegation) and the first session almost foundered before it began. What emerges from this situation is the difficulty which the Vatican administration has in being sensitive to the real concerns and interests of the Orthodox *outside* the rather limited sphere of self-consciously ecumenical activities. Coordination of policy and language across the whole range of Curial activities will be essential if an impression of double-dealing is to be avoided.

tive of the deepest life and thought of both churches remains to be seen.[4]

The Church, the Eucharist and the Trinity

Let us examine now the first statement produced by the Joint Theological Commission: "The Mystery of the Church and of the Eucharist in the Light of the Mystery of the Holy Trinity." We should recognize first of all that it does not have the authority of any synod behind it; it is not "official" teaching in either the Orthodox or the Roman Catholic sense of that term. At the same time its importance should not be minimized—there has been nothing quite like it produced by Orthodox and Roman Catholics in over five hundred years.

The document deals in three chapters or sections with three questions put before the Joint Commission at its first meeting in 1980: 1) How is the sacramental nature of the Church and Eucharist to be understood in relation to Christ and the Holy Spirit? (dealt with in Section 1 of the document); 2) How does the *local* Church's celebration of the Eucharist centered on the bishop relate to the mystery of the *one* God in *three* Persons? (dealt with in Section 2); 3) What is the relationship between this Eucharistic celebration of the *local* Church and the communion of *all* local churches in the *one,* holy Church of the one God in three Persons? (dealt with in Section 3). We will call attention now to certain passages in the document of particular interest to our own concerns here.

---

[4] Consider the following views expressed by a council of Athonite monks: "From the Orthodox point of view there is no justification for optimism in regard to the dialogue, and for this reason no haste should be exhibited concerning it. The Roman Catholics are pressing the dialogue, hoping to strengthen themselves by annexing Orthodoxy to themselves, for they are confronted by very powerful internal disturbances and crises, as is well known. The number of former Roman Catholics who have converted to Orthodoxy also disturbs them. But Orthodoxy has no reason to hasten towards dialogue since the papists remain so obdurate and immovable as regards infallibility, uniatism, and the rest of their pernicious teachings.

Hastening the dialogue under such conditions is equivalent to spiritual suicide for the Orthodox. Many facts give the impression that the Roman Catholics are preparing a union on the pattern of a *unia*. Can it be that the Orthodox who are hastening to the dialogue are conscious of this?" In same document the monks speak of the weakness and insufficiency of the Orthodox delegation; cf. "Documentation: The Announcement of the Extraordinary Joint Conference of the Sacred Community of the Holy Mount Athos concerning dialogue between the Orthodox and Roman Catholics," *Diakonia,* 16 (1981) 80-82, citation on p. 82.

Catholic-Orthodox Dialogue: Present Position 63

Section 1

In trying to answer how Church and Eucharist are to be understood in relation to Christ and the Holy Spirit, the Commission begins by observing that from Pentecost to the Parousia, the time of the Eighth Day, what God has done in Christ (the "Christ event") is given to us to experience through material and created realities (1.1). The Eucharist, Christ's Body and Blood "given" for us, exists as the "sacrament of Christ himself," and so an identity is established between the ultimate sacrament, which is Christ himself, and the sacrament of the Holy Eucharist whereby we are incorporated into Christ (1.2).

There then follows a characteristic and significant passage:

> The incarnation of the Son of God, his death and resurrection were realized from the beginning, according to the Father's will, in the Holy Spirit. This Spirit, which proceeds eternally from the Father and manifests himself through the Son, prepared the Christ event and realized it fully in the resurrection. Christ, who is the sacrament *par excellence,* given by the Father for the world, continues to give himself for the many in the Spirit, who alone gives life (Jn 6)). The sacrament of Christ is also a reality which can only exist in the Spirit (1.3).

The passage is characteristic because of the emphasis it places on the activity of the Holy Spirit. This emphasis is of course familiar to Eastern Christian theology but it has been recovered more and more in our own day in the West also. The presence of this emphasis in the document is not to be interpreted as the "victory" of one side over the other, but as an example of the "en-joy-ment" of the fullness of the Tradition which is sometimes preserved more adequately in the East and sometimes in the West. The work of the Spirit is described more completely in 1.5.a-d where the Holy Spirit is said to *prepare* the coming of Christ, to *manifest* Christ in his work as Savior, to *transform* the sacred gifts into the Body and Blood of Christ, and to *put into communion* with the body of Christ those who share the same bread and the same cup. In 1.4.a and 1.5 these activities of the Spirit are termed "energies," a clear and conscious allusion to the Trinitarian terminology of the Christian East.[5]

The passage cited above from Section 1.3 and another passage from

---

[5] 1.4.a: "The Eucharist and the church, body of the crucified and risen Christ, become the place of the energies of the the Holy Spirit." I.5: "The celebration of the eucharist reveals the divine energies manifested by the Spirit at work in the body of Christ."

Section 1.6 are the closest that the document comes to raising the problem of the *Filioque*.[6] It is to be noted that the language is more Eastern than Western in its reference to the "manifestation" of the Spirit through the Son (rather then the *procession* of Spirit from the Son) and in its reference to the Father as "the sole source in the Trinity." This wording does not technically exclude the Western understanding of relations within the Trinity, but it is certainly weighted on the Orthodox side. These observations are important because we are dealing precisely with a *common* statement. Such statements tend to be "filled in" with the differing undestandings of the respectives sides and much frustration and disappointment is produced unless people realize that exactly the same words can resonate quite differently in different ears. Awareness of this problem is at least a first major step in dealing fruitfully with documents of this kind. The unraveling of the agreement reached at Florence in 1439 warns us not to forget this difficulty.

A last important theme broached in Section 1 is the action of the Holy Spirit in the Eucharist. I wish to discuss this under two headings, the nature of the Church and the meaning of the Eucharistic epiclesis.

We read in Section 1.5.d:

> The Spirit puts into communion with the body of Christ those who share the same bread and the same cup. Starting from there, the Church manifests what it is, the sacrament of the Trinitarian *koinonia*, the "dwelling of God with men" (cf. Rev 21.4).

This claim—that the communion in the Church through the Eucharist is the work of the Spirit—is of fundamental importance for the future of the dialogue because it raises perhaps the most basic question of all: do Roman Catholics and Orthodox consider one another to be members of the Church?

This may seem a rather simple question, but it demands attention. On the Roman Catholic side, at least since the *Decree on Ecumenism* of Vatican II, the answer has been clear. The Orthodox Church possesses true sacraments which include not only baptism, but also—through the apostolic succession—holy orders and Eucharist. For Roman Catholics,

---

[6]1.6: "Without wishing to resolve yet the difficulties which have arisen between the East and the West concerning the relationship between the Son and the Spirit, we can already say together that this Spirit, which proceeds from the Father (Jn 15.26) as the sole source in the Trinity and which has become the Spirit of our sonship (Rom 8.15) since he is also the Spirit of the Son (Gal 4.6), is communicated to us particularly in the Eucharist by this Son upon whom he reposes in time and in eternity" (Jn 1.32).

then, this document from the Joint Commission will be understood to assert the the *koinonia*/communion effected by the Holy Spirit in the Eucharist is the *same* communion for both Roman Catholics and for Orthodox: an identical reality proceeding from a single source. As the document says: "The Spirit puts into communion with the body of Christ those who share the same bread and the same cup" (1.5.d).

On the Orthodox side, however, it is not at all so clear that the Orthodox Church plainly accepts the *ecclesial* reality of Roman Catholicism. Orthodox ecclesiology and sacramental theology achieved no definitive formulation during the period of the Seven Ecumenical Synods, and since that time there have been many different approaches, both in theory and fact, when dealing with those whom (like Roman Catholics) the Orthodox tradition considers heretical. No authoritative statement exists in the Orthodox world which recognized that Roman Catholics are members of the Church of Christ in the strict theological sense and that their sacraments (including the Eucharist) are therefore sacraments *of* the Church. Many individual Orthodox certainly believe that this is the case, and many gestures by Orthodox leaders and hierarchs seem to imply this belief, but this view can always be regarded as a personal opinion only and, moreover, as an opinion which does not necessarily reflect the true position of Orthodoxy. Such is clearly the approach of the monks of Mount Athos.

Here is obviously a delicate matter. If Roman Catholics *press* for this kind of clear theological recognition of their ecclesial reality (a reality which they themselves have already accorded to the Orthodox Church), then there is a great risk that the spirit of collaboration and consensus which has only become a practical reality among Orthodox themselves in the last few decades will break apart again under the strain of this unresolved issue. On the other hand, the dialogue itself will plunge further and further into unreality if these glowing theological statements are perceived by Roman Catholics as applying to them in a hypothetical manner: "*If* you belong to the Church (in the strict theological sense), *then* your Eucharist is indeed all these things we have agreed upon." I close this difficult but crucial point by quoting the words of Father Theodore Stylianopoulos of the Holy Cross Greek Orthodox School of Theology in Brookline, Massachusetts:

> The Orthodox need to find a way to accept the principle that officially recognizing ecclesial reality in other Christian bodies neither is an affront to the Orthodox Church as the one, holy, catholic, and apostolic Church, nor necessitates sacramental communion with

them. Acceptance of this principle would then relieve the Orthodox position from the heavy burden of virtually denying that other people in the world are Christians.[7]

The other dimension of the work of the Holy Spirit in the Eucharist has to do with the Eucharistic epiclesis. This matter is raised in a pointed way in Section 1.6:

> That is why the eucharistic mystery is accomplished in the prayer which joins together the words by which the word made flesh instituted the sacrament and the *epiclesis* in which the Church, moved by faith, entreats the Father, through the Son, to send the Spirit so that in the unique offering of the incarnate Son, everything may be consummated in unity.

The passage is significant because it transcends the context of previous discussion about the precise moment of consecration in the Eucharist: the words of institution according to Western tradition; the epiclesis of the Holy Spirit upon the Gifts according to Eastern tradition. The document proposes no theory about the Eucharistic consecration and does not choose between the older approaches. Instead the whole meaning of epiclesis is deepened and the temptation to choose between Christ and the Spirit in the understanding of the Eucharist is rejected, a positive step towards recovering the fullness of tradition in the Eucharist:

> The Spirit transforms the sacred gifts into the body and blood of Christ (*metabole*) in order to bring about the growth of the body which is the church. In this sense the entire celebration is an *epiclesis*, which becomes more explicit at certain moments. The Church is continually in a state of *epiclesis* (1.5.c).

Section 2

With Section 2 the document begins to explore a certain *mystical* identity/analogy between the life of the Church (understood as the "sacrament of Christ") and the mystery of the Trinity itself.

Section 2.1 speaks in these terms:

> Now the Church existing in a place is not formed, in a radical sense,

---

[7] Theodore Stylianopoulos, "Orthodoxy and Catholicism: A New Attempt at Dialogue," *The Greek Orthodox Theological Review*, 26 (1981) 157-69 at p. 164.

by the persons who come together to establish it. There is a "Jerusalem from on high" which "comes down from God," a communion which is at the foundation of the community itself. The Church comes into being by a free gift, that of the new creation.

The text here presents a radical change to the idea that the Church is adequately understood by beginning from the visible/sociological reality. Instead we are invited to consider the "gift of God," the "new creation," phrases which inevitably lead the mind to Jesus' own words in John 4.10, "If you knew the gift of God . . . " and to the identification of God's gift with the person of the Holy Spirit himself (Acts 2.38; 8.20; 10.45).

> This mystery of the unity in love of many persons constitutes the real newness of the Trinitarian *koinonia* communicated to men in the Church through the eucharist. . . . This is why the Church finds its model, its origin and its purpose in the mystery of God, one in three Persons (2.1)

The Trinity is thus of central importance for Christians here and now and not just at the "end" of all things. This emphasis is plainly of the fruits of Orthodox/Roman Catholic collaboration and provides a valuable counterweight (whatever the merits or demerits of this particular text) to the prevailing enthusiasm for "theological anthropology" as the only acceptable method for theologians today.

The text goes on to speak of the bishop's ministry within this Eucharistic and Trinitarian vision of the Church:

> By the sacrament of ordination the Spirit of the Lord "confers" on the bishop, not juridically as if it were a pure transmission of power, but sacramentally, the authority of servant which the Son received from the Father and which he received in a human way by his acceptance in his passion.
>
> The bishop stands at the heart of the local church as minister of the Spirit to discern the charisms and take care that they are exercised in harmony, for the good of all, in faithfulness to the apostolic tradition.
>
> The union of the community with him [the bishop] is first of all of the order of *mysterion* and not primordially of the juridical order (2.3).

The bishop is presented here as the servant of ecclesial unity, but a unity conceived not as merely a human consensus or collaboration, but itself as a *mysterion*, a sacrament of that communion which is the very life of the divine Persons. The text shows a strong desire to deepen the view of the episcopal ministry, since, in different ways, both Roman Catholics and Eastern Orthodox are tempted to treat the bishop's role too much in terms of external authority: canons and privileges and power. The emphasis on the sacramentality of the office is a welcome one, and Catholics may be forgiven if they find that the Commission's description of the bishop's task ("to discern the charisms and take care that they are exercised in harmony, for the good of all" 2.3) seems to them to describe very well what they understand the role of the Papacy to be in the life of the visible Church as a whole.

Section 3

The last section of the document explores the relation between the local church and the reality of the whole Church as the Body of Christ. The characteristic terms of this exploration are found in 3.1:

> The identity of one eucharistic assembly with another comes from the fact that all with the same faith celebrate the same memorial, that all by eating the same bread and sharing in the same cup become the same unique body of Christ into which they have been integrated by the same baptism. If there are many celebrations, there is nevertheless only one mystery celebrated in which all participate.
>
> In the same way, the local church which celebrates the Eucharist gathered around its bishop is not a section of the Body of Christ. The multiplicity of local synaxes does not divide the Church, but rather shows sacramentally its unity.

Here is expressed very succintly that "eucharistic ecclesiology" developed in this century by Orthodox theologians such as the late Nicolas Afanassieff and Professor John Zizioulas (a member of the Joint Commission representing the Ecumenical Patriarchate). At the core of this understanding of the Church lies a series of "identities" that are manifested in and through one another. The eucharistic Body of the Lord, the local eucharistic community as Body, the entire Church as a communion of eucharistic communities each recognizing its own mystical identity at the heart of the other—all of these together do not make up some composite "whole" consisting of separate parts. Rather, each is found wholly in the other and manifests in itself the same reality which is found in all.

We find then among these [local] churches those bonds of communion which the New Testament indicated: communion in faith, hope and love, communion in the sacraments, communion in the diversity of charisms, communion in the reconciliation, communion in the ministry. The agent of this communion is the Spirit of the risen Lord (3.4).

Once again the imagery of communion, in this case the "bonds" of love (Eph 4.3; Col 3.14), rejoins the traditional imagery Christians have always used for the action of the Holy Spirit as *vinculum amoris,* the bond of love.

From this vision of the Church as communion flows another vision of the bishop's oversight as it is exercised within the Church. Here the language of the document reproduces almost exactly the language of the *Dogmatic Constitution on the Church* from Vatican II:

> [the bishops] have in common the same responsibility and the same service to the Church. Because the one and only Church is made present in his local church, each bishop cannot separate the care for his own church from that of the universal Church. When, by the sacrament of ordination, he receives the charism of the Spirit for the *episkope* of one local church, his own, by that very fact he receives the charism of the Spirit for the *episkope* of the entire Church.
>
> The *episkope* for the universal Church is seen to be entrusted by the Spirit to the totality of local bishops in communion with one another. This commuion is expressed traditionally through conciliar practice. We shall have to examine further the way it is conceived and realized in the perspective of what we have just explained (3.4).

That last section of the text shows clearly the Commission's awareness that the main point of disagreement between the Roman Catholic and Orthodox traditions, namely, the place of the Pope in the life of the Church, cannot be left to one side for too long, no matter how hard the members try to stick to what is common to both traditions.

Let me end this part of our reflections by taking note of some criticisms that have already been made of the Commission's first document. It has been said, for example, that the whole approach is too abstract or, more precisely, too *idealized.* Use of the language of the Body of Christ may leave no room for the image of the Church as the "People of God" (warts and all), a language central to Roman Catholic reflection since Vatican II. Observers have pointed out that references to the "sinfulness" of the visible Church had to be "put in" afterwards at the time of revision. This criticism of the document has some validity with respect to the style of the text, but there is no reason why texts like the present one have to sound like everything else that is being written today. The only real question is whether the emphasis placed on "Body" distorts or betrays in some way other truths about the Church.

The criticism has also been advanced that the language of the document is more "impressionistic" than it is theologically precise. This criticism touches on the pervasive language of *identity* which insists that the personal body of Christ, the sacramental Body in the Eucharist and the ecclesial Body are the same reality. It may well be that this affirmation of the uniqueness and identity of the Body in its various manifestations can lead us to overlook what is particular to each mode. If this is a danger it can be addressed by the Commission in its future work. A similar problem may attach to the way the document speaks of *communion* with regard to the Trinity. A strongly paradoxical approach seems to be taken at times which suggests that the unity of the Godhead consists precisely in the very fact of the diversity of the Persons. It is not clear that this paradoxical sense is true to the Trinitarian tradition of either the West or the East, and, when transferred as a model to the communion of the Church, it might seem to give a positive theological meaning to differences that have not been treated positively by Christians before.

Local Implications for Roman Catholics and Orthodox

We have looked quickly at some of the more interesting aspects of the first common Orthodox/Roman Catholic theological document. By way of conclusion let us try to relate this and Catholic/Orthodox relations as a whole to our own situation here in Toronto.

Every student of Orthodox/Roman Catholic affairs always points to the primacy of the life of the Church in Orthodox experience, and therefore to the crucial importance of getting the Orthodox *faithful*— not just the theologians and bishops—to understand and support the movement towards unity. Orthodox believers themselves will be the ultimate arbiters of the dialogue and of any steps towards unity which the Commission may propose. This was true after the Council of Florence and it is probably still true today; nothing will happen "over the heads" of the people.

The same may not be exactly true (or true in exactly the same way) on the Roman Catholic side, but ignorance and indifference towards the East on the part of Roman Catholics has been in the past and can still be in the future a deadening weight that drains the life out any movement towards rediscovery and reunion. What then is to be done? The question becomes even more acute if we take the Commission's insistence on the theological importance of the local Church as a cue for us to consider our own situation here with some realism.

Toronto, for all its many merits and glories, is *not* the center of the theological world, and so it is unlikely that what happens here, among us, is going to have dramatic effects at the level of the theological discussions we have been examining this evening. As Saint Paul might have said, "not many of us are wise . . . not many are powerful" (cf. 1 Cor 1.26). Moreover, the circumstances of the local Orthodox communities in Toronto also make it difficult for them to be active in the usual forms of ecumenical activity. They have mostly arrived in the recent past and as yet have no theological schools, no seminaries in Canada to meet their *own* needs, let alone provide an endless stream of speakers and debaters to dialogue with other churches. On the other hand, the search for Christian unity is not a spectator sport. We are not meant to watch (except in the biblical sense of "watch and pray"), but to take part. How is this to be done?

One way is to realize that locally we are still at the stage of the dialogue of *love*. We need to create a network of prayer, personal contacts and deep charity that can sustain the weight of the discussions that even now we *do* have, as in a forum like the Saint Peter and Saint Andrew Lectures. There are two sides to this dialogue of love, however, that I would like to recommend to your prayers and your attention.

The first of these is what Patriarch Athenagoras and Pope Paul VI referred to as a "purification of memories." This phrase was used of the lifting of the excommunications of 1054 and appeals for the purging of that weight of bitterness which has collected from the past. This purging of bitterness perhaps demands more of Orthodox than of Catholics, because it is true in general that Eastern Christians have more to forgive and forget in the long history of East/West relations. Roman Catholics probably need a "jogging" of memories as much as they need a purification of memories, but the object of the challenge is not to wallow in guilt for past injustices. We are meant instead to plunge our roots more deeply into the history of the undivided Church and recover that first and fresh sense of communion between East and West. This is demanded of us in a special way because we live in a *new* country, a country and a society still in the process of formation. We are called to rid our memories of the resentments and grudges of the past and to provide for the generations to come *memories* of a deeper past which can nourish rather than poison the future. This is a duty laid upon Roman Catholics and Orthodox alike.

The second side to this dialogue of love that is open to all of us in Toronto is to dedicate ourselves to the renewal of our *own* churches, to become as deeply and generously and honestly Orthodox or Catholic as we can be. The dialogue of love *and* the dialogue of truth have nothing whatever to fear from those who have come to know and live their own traditions and have assimilated them into their very bones. It is the armchair ecumenist and the armchair critic who is to be feared, like the withered tree in the first psalm. The work of Christian unity is a work of faith and perseverance; there are no half-hour solutions like the kind handed out on television programs. If this work is to flourish among us, we all need to have our roots plunged into the living water of Christ's own *life*.

Conclusion

I would like to finish with two images. The first image is one of *metanoia* or conversion, of turning things around. It lies behind some wise words spoken by Metropolitan Damaskenos of Tranoupolis: "We shouldn't only be asking: 'Do we each have the right to give communion to one another?', but we should also ask: 'Do we each have the right to *refuse* communion to one another?' "[8] The Metropolitan's words are by no means a plea for instant inter-communion between Orthodox and Roman Catholics, but they *are* a plea nevertheless, a plea to stand our normal, rather comfortable vision of the Church on its head, to "turn things around" so that we can see what the Spirit of God would have us see.

The second image is one of hope and I take it from the Letter of Ephesians 4.12-13. The Apostle says that the different gifts in the Church have been distributed by Christ "for the equipment of the saints" (πρὸς τὸν καταρτισμὸν τῶν ἁγίων), for the work of ministry, for building up the body of Christ, until we all attain to the unity of the faith and the knowledge of the Son of God." We are equipped then, and the equipment we have been given is to be put to work to attain "the unity of the faith"—even in our own time, even in Toronto.

---

[8] Metr. Damaskenos Papandreou, "L'unité dans la diversité: le point de vue orthodoxe," *La Documentation Catholique*, 79 (1982) 2 March 1982, Nr. 1829, 473-78 at p. 478.

Feminist Theology: An Orthodox Christian Perspective

DEBORAH BELONICK

Saint Irenaios of Lyons wrote: "The glory of God is a living human, and the life of humanity is the vision of God."[1] Theologians are constantly aware of these two realities—God and humanity—and their task is to discover and define the relationship between the two. How does the Θεός, the All-seeing, view creatures, and how do creatures in turn view God? Who is this Being with whom in the beginning of salvation history we walked in the Garden of Paradise? Who are we, whom God looked upon and viewed as "very good" (Gen 1.31)?

These are the questions which are of import to all theologians. The answers to them shape our faith, our present worldview and our expectations of life after death. In short, what we believe about God and ourselves shapes our lifestyles, our activities, our moral decisions. It ultimately also affects our salvation. If we correctly interpret ourselves and the Deity, we are open to grace and the Spirit of God. If we misinterpret these two objective realities, we open ourselves to delusion and darkness; we lose the opportunity for salvation. If we follow false anthropological or theological concepts, we lose an I/Thou relationship with God grounded in reality.

It is for these reasons that "theologies" must constantly and consistently be checked. What I think might be especially profitable today is to check some tenets of a current popular theology, feminist theology, regarding concepts for God and human beings. Is it a theology guiding our era toward a true γνῶσις of God and ourselves? To answer, I will present a traditional overview of humanity and the Trinity from Scripture and the writings of the early Church, which will provide a backdrop by which feminist theology may be questioned. As an Orthodox Christian

---

[1] *Against Heresies* 4.20.7, PG 7.1037B. Irenaios was writing in the last quarter of the second century.

woman, I believe wholeheartedly that the tradition of the Church provides us with objective, pertinent information through which we can arrive at a vision of God and humanity given by the Spirit of God.

The Significance of Gender in Creation

According to the words of Saint Paul in his letters to the Galatians and Corinthians, women and men of the Christian community have equal access to union with God through their baptism in the name of Jesus Christ as well as in the fruits of the Holy Spirit (Gal 3.28; 1 Cor 12.4-31; Gal 5.22). Orthodox Christians believe that the prophecy of Joel (2.28-29) has come to pass and that God indeed has poured out his spirit upon his maidservants and menservants. Both women and men have been given the possibility of union with God, or θέωσις, as the Orthodox say. A hymn at the feast of Pentecost expresses this glorification of humanity filled with the Spirit of God: "The Holy Spirit is light and life, a living fountain of knowledge . . . God, and making us God."

However, this prophetical fulfillment and possibility for θέωσις in no way excludes gender distinction. Orthodox dogma includes the belief that both in creation and redemption, God wills gender distinction.

This dogma opposes current, particularly feminist theology, which often adheres to the hope that in the realm of God, all gender distinction finally will be abolished. I quote from Eleanor McLaughlin and Rosemary Radford Ruether in their book, *Women of Spirit*:

> . . . through holiness and ecstasy a woman transcends "nature" and participates in the eschatological sphere. She anticipates the order of salvation in heaven. In this eschatological order sexual hierarchy is abolished for that asexual personhood in which there is "neither male nor female."[2]

Many other contemporary theologians agree with McLaughlin and Ruether in the premise that gender distinction is *only* anatomical, relatively insignificant and a passing creaturely mode expressive of fallen humanity. The Orthodox separate themselves from this current theology on all points, considering gender distinction to be psychological as well as anatomical, significant to being human, and a mode willed in creation and present in the realm of God.

The stories of Genesis are good starting points for these Orthodox

[2](New York, 1979), p. 23.

dogmas. Consider Genesis 1.27: "So God created man in his own image, in the image of God he created him; male and female he created them." In the Hebrew text the word for "man" is *adam*. "*Adam* is therefore not only the name of the first man, but also of man in general. . . . Further on in Genesis it is said that God gave the name . . . *Adam* to both man and woman. . . . Since the Holy Scriptures call the first man simply 'man' (*adam*), does this not suggest that he was created first without sex? Or, perhaps, that he contained both sexes within himself, was an androgynous being? The Book of Genesis dismisses this notion by saying that God created man as 'male and female.' The words *zakar* and *neqebah* are used here in the Hebrew text, which mean 'man' and 'woman' precisely in the sexual sense. (In Hebrew these words may be used equally well in reference to male and female animals.) Nowhere in Holy Scriptures is there a trace of the idea of sexlessness or hermaphroditic nature of Adam (This idea did appear in the later theology of Judaism)."[3]

Genesis 2.18 further emphasizes the gender distintions between woman and man, stating: "It is not good that the man should be alone; I will make a helper fit for him." "Helper fit" (in Hebrew, *eser kenegdo*) implies ". . . counterpart, a mirror, a person created to help man discover himself. Scripture implies, therefore, that the woman is not a passive or inferior force, but the other half necessary for a mutually enriching dialogue."[4] "Helper fit" implies as well a psychological complementarity between female and male.

All of the Genesis narratives, including the terms *ish* and *ishshah* in Genesis 2.23, emphasize not only the common humanity of woman and man but also the fact that human existence is dimorphic. All texts preceding the story of the Fall denote the commonality of women and men, plus their psychological and anatomical distinctiveness.

Many contemporary female authors—in various sciences—are advocating the recognition of this dimorphic state of humanity. Within their fields, they are trying to formulate what is expressed by the Spirit in Genesis.[5] One example is scientist Diane Desimone who states from

---

[3]Sergius Verhovskoy, "Creation of Man and the Establishment of the Family in the Light of the Book of Genesis," *St. Vladimir's Seminary Quarterly*, 8 (1964) 5-30 at pp. 5-10.

[4]Joan Schaupp, *Woman: Image of the Holy Spirit* (Denville, N.J., 1975), pp. 72-73.

[5]Jo Durden-Smith and Diane DeSimone, *Sex and the Brain* (New York, 1983); Carol Gilligan, *In a Different Voice: Psychological Theory and Women's Development* (Cambridge, Mass., 1982); Hilda G. Graef, *The Scholar and the Cross: The Life and Work of Edith Stein* (Westminster, Md., 1955); Helen M. Luke, *Woman, Earth and Spirit: The Feminine in Symbol and Myth* (New York, 1981); Joan Schaupp, *Woman: Image of the Holy Spirit* (Denville, N.J., 1975).

her research (with Jo Durden-Smith): "Sex is a *major* dimension of human difference ... further these differences appear as independent of culture ... men are more 'rule-bound' in solving problems, less sensitive to situational variables, more narrowly focused, more persevering. ... Women are *very* sensitive to context, good at picking up peripheral information, and processing information faster."[6]

The Permanent Character of Gender Distinction

In traditional Scriptural interpretation, the human being is known to be comprised of body and soul. J. Pederson, in his work, *Israel*, goes so far as to say: "... [in Hebrew thought] soul and body are so intimately united that a distinction cannot be made between them. They are more than 'united;' the body is the soul in its outward form."[7]

This Hebrew concept endured through the early centuries of the Church, and is present in the Orthodox Church today. Saint Irenaios acknowledged that the perfect human was a union of soul and body, vivified by the Spirit of God: "... the perfect man consists in the conmingling and the union of the soul receiving the Spirit of the Father, and admixture of that fleshly nature which was molded after the image of God."[8] Anatomy is not merely a concession of God given for procreation.[9] Rather, anatomical image is related to the soul, making the person an integrated whole. In the fourth century, Saint Gregory of Nyssa restated the dogma that the soul is the inward image of the body.[10]

Further, the tragedy of a human being encountering Death was (and is to the Orthodox) that this soul-body correlation and union is destroyed; the person is de-humanized by Death because the body separates from the soul and decomposes. "Do the shades of Sheol rise up to praise

---

[6] *Sex and the Brain*, pp. 54 and 59.

[7] Vol. 1 (London/Copenhagen, 1926), p. 171.

[8] *Against Heresies* 5.6.1, PG 7.1137A.

[9] Many writings in the Eastern patristic tradition in fact state that the dimorphic character of humanity was created in prevision of the Fall, for the purpose of procreation. These tendencies to view humanity as essentially "spiritual" beings trapped in carnal bodies for the sole purpose of procreation began with the Jewish philosopher Philo and reappeared in Eastern Fathers such as Saint John Damascene, Saint Gregory of Nyssa, Saint John Chrysostom (who later changed his mind on the matter) and Saint Maximos the Confessor. However, this notion is not acceptable as being compatible with the dogmas and main Tradition of the Orthodox Church. See John Meyendorff, *Christ in Eastern Christian Thought* (Crestwood, N.Y., 1975) pp. 232-33, n. 28.

[10] *Dialogue on the Soul and Resurrection*, PG 46.72C-76B and cf. *On the Creation of Man* 27, PG 44.225B-C.

Thee?" wails the Psalmist (Ps 88.10). Georges Florovsky, a contemporary Orthodox theologian, reiterates:

> Neither soul nor body separately represents man. A body without a soul is but a corpse, and a soul without a body is a ghost. . . . This organic wholeness . . . was from the very beginning strongly emphasized by all Christian teachers. That is why the separation of soul and body is the death of the man himself, the discontinuation of his existence, of wholeness, i.e. of his existence as a man. Consequently, death and the corruption of the body are a sort of fading away of the 'image of God' in man.[11]

In regard to the resurrection of the dead, the Orthodox Christian hopes for the reunion of the body with the soul, and that both soul and body will be vivified by the Holy Spirit of God. Saint Paul expressed this to the church at Corinth: " . . . not that we would be unclothed, but that we would be further clothed, so that what is mortal may be swallowed up by life" (2 Cor 5.4). Gender distinction, willed by God as "very good," will remain in the eschatological realm. Saint Jerome succinctly stated:

> If the woman shall not rise again as a woman, nor the man as a man, there will be no resurrection of the dead . . . if there shall be no resurrection of the body, there can be no resurrection of the dead.[12]

Clearly, there are major anthropological discrepancies between current feminist thought and the tradition of the early Church. Clearly, too, salvation is contigent upon which system of thought one chooses. Belief in the traditional anthropology leads one to integral beauty and deification which reaches its fulfillment in union with Christ after death. Belief in feminist anthropology leads one to a disintegrated existence much akin to the state hoped for by Platonic philosophers.[13] Christian salvation demands choosing the traditional view over the feminist view, and subsequently demands ordering our world justly in accordance with it—avoiding the creation of stereotypical categories for women yet not departing from the creative and redemptive significance of gender wrought by Jesus Christ. When speaking of justice for women, I favor a

---

[11]"Redemption," in his *Collected Works*, vol. 3: *Creation and Redemption* (Belmont, Mass., 1976), pp. 106-07.

[12]*Letter 108 to the Virgin Eustochia* 23 (22), PL 22.900. The letter was written in 404 A.D.

[13]Florovsky, "Redemption," p. 111.

quote from Edith Stein: "For not every kind of conduct displaying consistency and constancy according to purely subjective principles constitutes the true character [of humanity] but perseverance in obeying the eternal principles of justice . . . perfect justice can exist only where the things of God are given to God, as is done by the true Christian."[14] The "things of God," according to Orthodox anthropology, include dimorphic human be-ing, and the value of it in the church community and in society at large.

Language for God

The vision of God, as expressed in language, is another discrepancy between feminist theology and the tradition of the Church which should be explored. It is imperative to explain the significance of the terms "Father, Son, and Holy Spirit" which have formed the traditional doxology of Christians since the manifestation of Jesus Christ in the world (Mk 1.9-11; 2 Cor 13.13). It is imperative that the Church explain its vision of God in addition to its vision of humanity.

It is a dogma of the Orthodox Christian Church that, in a sense, all efforts to name God are inadequate, since God is transcendent and essentially unknowable. Even on the feast of Epiphany when Orthodox Christians celebrate the revelation of God as Trinity, they are reminded of this in the hymnography of the Church: "Great are Thou, O Lord, and marvelous are Thy works: no words suffice to sing the praise of Thy wonders."[15] Both Scripture and the patristic writings echo this transcendence of the Deity. Solomon, in the Book of Kings (1 Kg 8.12) says that God desires to "dwell in thick darkness" beyond the comprehension of human beings. Saint Gregory of Nyssa spoke of the impossibility of adequately describing God: "This inability to give expression to such unutterable things, while it reflects upon the poverty of our own nature, affords an evidence of God's glory, teaching us as it does, in the words of the Apostle, that the only name naturally appropriate to God is to believe Him to be "above every

---

[14]A Jewish woman who converted to Roman Catholicism, became a nun (Sister Benedicta a Cruce in the Carmelite Order), and died in a Nazi concentration camp in World War II. Stein, a phenomenologist and religious who wrote much about feminine character, advocated that each woman develop her wholeness by constantly developing her humanity, her individuality, *and* her femininity. See Edith Stein, "Problems of Women's Education," in *Writings of Edith Stein,* ed. and trans. Hilda G. Graef (Westminster, Md., 1956), pp. 126-60 at p. 147.

[15]Hymn at the Blessing of Water on Epiphany.

name" (Phil 2.9)."[16] Our inability to name God exactly is evidence of God's transcendence.

On the other hand, creatures do employ a myriad of terms in attempts to name God, and this is evidence of God's immanence. The hymnography of the Orthodox Church expresses this also in its exclamation that "God is the Lord and has revealed himself unto us."[17] Again, Scripture and the patristic writings concur; creatures do have access to words relevant to God. Saint John the Theologian writes in his gospel: "No one has ever seen God; the only Son, who is in the bosom of the Father, he has made him known" (Jn 1.18). Saint Clement of Alexandria (2nd century) explains that by revelation humans are able to call God Just, Good, Mind, One, Lord, Rock, Love, *et cetera*, yet all these terms "are not to be taken in their strict meaning . . . we use these appellations of honor, in order that our thought may have something to rest on and not to wander at random. . . . "[18] Saint Gregory of Nyssa further notes:

> metaphors innumerable are taken from human life to illustrate symbolically divine things. As, then, each of the names [for God] has a human sound but not a human meaning . . . [they hide] a distinction between the uttered meanings exactly proportionate to the differences existing between the subjects of this title.[19]

In short, any human word used to describe or to name the Deity can be only an approximate description. In his essence, God remains unknowable; the distance between the creature and the Divine remains. God is ineffable and incomprehensible.[20] Human words never can describe the Deity fully but seek only to express as much as God has revealed, and to keep our minds from "wandering at random." All human language remains metaphorical.

Nevertheless, despite their realizations about the shortcomings of

---

[16] *Against Eunomios* 12, PG 45.1108B-C.

[17] Hymn from the Service of Matins in the Orthodox Church.

[18] *Stromata* 5.12.82, PG 9.121B.

[19] *Against Eunomios* 1.39, PG 45.444A-B.

[20] It is an Orthodox dogma that God remains unknowable in "essence," that abyss of Divinity which forever is transcendent and unknowable. What is revealed to humanity are God's "energies" (in Western terms: "attributes"). Pseudo-Dionysios calls these revelations from God "super-essential rays of the divine darkness" (cf. *The Mystical Theology* 1.1, PG 3.1000A-C). God bursts forth from hiding to communicate with human beings, to reveal something of the Deity; Vladimir Lossky, *In the Image and Likeness of God* (Crestwood, N.Y., 1974), p. 41.

human language, the patristic writers did not fail to insist that some revealed metaphors were superior to others. It is within this superior, precise category that the personal terms "Father, Son, and Holy Spirit" fell. A close reading of patristic texts explains why.

There were two fourth-century theologians, Saint Athanasios and Saint Gregory of Nyssa, who were embroiled in controversies over the proper terms for God. Their disputes are worthwhile for study, given feminist accusations that traditional doxologies have deified "maleness" and have been non-inclusive toward women.

Athanasios was defending the traditional trinitarian names against the Arians, a group which called the first person of the Trinity "Creator" rather than "Father." Arians claimed that Jesus Christ was not the Son of God but merely a superior creature; therefore "Father" was a fleshly, foolish, improper term for God. In reply to the Arians, Athanasios tried to illustrate the importance of the biblical divine names "Father, Son, and Holy Spirit."

Using a term such as "Creator," said Athanasios, makes God dependent on creatures for his existence. If creation did not exist, he asked, would this "Creator-God" cease to be? If creation had never existed, what would be the proper term for God?

In addition, he argued, the word "Creator" could be used to describe *any* of the members of the Trinity. It would be wrong to refer to the Father alone as " Creator" because the Bible states:

> In the beginning God created the heavens and earth. The earth was without form and void, and darkness was upon the face of the deep; and the *Spirit of God* was moving over the face of the waters (Gen 1.1-2).

> In the beginning was the Word, and the Word was with God, and the Word was God. He was in the beginning with God; *all things were made through him*, and without him was not anything made that was made (Jn 1.1-3).

In Orthodox Christian thought, and according to Scripture, the Trinity acts in concert. They all create; they all save (Jn 5.21; Acts 2.24; Rom 1.4); they all sanctify (Eph 5.26; 1 Thess 5.23). Athanasios argued that the names of God had to describe more than God's will or action toward creation. There are, in fact, two different sets of names which may be used for God according to Athanasios. One set [Creator, Savior, Sanctifier] refers to God's deeds or acts—that is, to his will and counsel— the other [Father, Son, Holy Spirit] to God's own essence and being.[21] Athanasios insisted that these two sets be formally and consistently distinguished. He insisted that one use the terms "Father, Son, and Holy Spirit" when speaking about the existence of God as three persons in a community of love, that is, when speaking about the relationships among members of the Trinity without regard to their economic acts toward creation. "God's 'Being' has an absolute ontological priority over God's action and will. . . . *God is much more than just 'Creator.' When we call God 'a Father' we mean something higher than his relation to creatures.*"[22]

Saint Gregory of Nyssa faced similar problems when dealing with a sect known as the Eunomians who believed that Christ was unlike God the Father by nature and instead was a created energy. For this reason the Eunomians refused to call God "Father." Gregory, appalled by this new teaching, sought to explain the character of the Holy Trinity, the relationships among the persons of the Trinity, and the Church's insistence upon the traditional terms "Father, Son, and Holy Spirit."

First, said Gregory, there was no more adequate theologian than the Lord himself who without compulsion or misdirection designated the Godhead as "Father, Son, and Holy Spirit."[23] Further, these names are not indications that God is a male or a man (Any Orthodox theologian would be shocked by such a deduction.) for God transcends human gender.[24] Rather, these names imply relationships among the persons of the Trinity, and distinguish them as separate persons who exist in a community of love. Even more crucial, the names lead one to contemplate the *correct* relationships among the three persons; they are clues to the inner life of the Trinity.

Gregory notes:

> For while there are many other names by which deity is indicated in the Historical Books, in the Prophets and in the Law, our Master Christ passes by all these and commits us to these titles as better able to bring us to the faith about the Self-Existent, declaring that it suffices us to cling to the titles, "Father, Son and Holy

---

[21]Georges Florovsky, "St. Athanasius' Concept of Creation," in his *Collected Works*, vol. 4: *Aspects of Church History* (Belmont, Mass., 1975), pp. 39-62 at p. 52.

[22]Ibid. (emphasis added) and cf. Athanasios, *Against Arians* 1.33, PG 26.80A-81A.

[23]*Against Eunomios* 2.9, PG 45.505A-516B.

[24]Gregory the Theologian also notes that the names of God have nothing whatever to do with human gender categories: *Homily* 31.7 (= *Theological Homily* 5), PG 36.140C-141A.

Spirit," in order to attain to the apprehension of him who is absolutely Existent, who is one and yet not one.[25]

Gregory states that it is with the terms "Father, Son, and Holy Spirit" that women and men can enter into the divine abyss, somewhat equipped to understand the inner relationships and Persons of the Trinity. He wrote a lengthy treatise on each term, explaining its connotations and relevance to Trinitarian life. Of particular interest in this era is Gregory's explanation of the term "Father," which is under scrutiny by feminist theologians as a harmful metaphor that resulted from a patriarchal church structure and culture. Gregory insists otherwise.

The name "Father," said Gregory, leads one to contemplate two things: a Being who is the source and cause of all; and that fact that this Being has a relationship with another Person—one can only be "Father" if there is a child involved.[26] Thus, the human term "Father" leads one naturally to think of another member of the Trinity, to contemplate more than is suggested by a term such as "Creator" or "Maker." By calling God "Father," Gregory notes, one understands that there exists with God a child from all eternity, a second Person who is co-ruling, coequal, and coeternal with God.[27] "Father" also connotes the initiator of a generation, the inaugurator of all, the one who begets life rather than conceiving it and bringing it to fruition in birth.[28] This is the mode of existence (the way of being) of the first Person of the Trinity. How he acts in trinitarian life is akin to the mode of a father in the earthly realm.

This divine Father is as different from and transcendent of earthly fathers as the divine is from the human. Nevertheless, it is *fatherhood* and not *motherhood* which describes his mode of life, his relationship to the second Person of the Trinity, and even his personal characteristics. The first Person of the Trinity does not just "act" like a father (though he sometimes acts like a mother!). Rather, his very being is divine

---

[25] Against Eunomios 2.2, PG 45.469A.

[26] *Against Eunomios* 2.2, PG 45.469B-D.

[27] Cf. *Against Eunomios* 4.1, PG 45.617A-628B.

[28] Feminists argue that woman, as well as man, is the source of all life, and therefore this first Person of the Holy Trinity may be called "Mother" as well as "Father." The early Church was well aware that both male and female cells were required to create life, and that the male was not the only source of life (John Chrysostom, *Homily on the Letter to the Ephesians* 20.4, *PG* 62.139-140. The Church, however, always maintained a distinction between begetting and bearing, between the male and female contributions and modes of action in creating life. The male cell is the generator, inaugurator and impregnator; there are distinctions within the basic biological act of creation.

fatherhood in a perfect fulfilled state. Fatherhood is a *function* of males on earth, but for the first person of the Trinity, it is the principle of his being.[29]

Clement of Alexandria expressed this idea most aptly: "God is himself love, and because of his love, he pursued us, and [in the eternal generation of the Son] the ineffable nature of God is father; his sympathy with us is mother."[30]

All sorts of epithets for God are available to humanity through revelation—goodness, love, mother, fire—but none are exchangeable for or comparable to the revelation of God as Father, Son, and Holy Spirit. These are the metaphors by which humanity enters trinitarian life to discover the unique persons of the Trinity and their distinguishable marks. The Liturgy of Saint John Chrysostom, used normally as the eucharistic service of the Orthodox Church, expresses this as well. Before the Lord's Prayer, the priest prays: "And grant us, O Lord, to dare to invoke Thee with confidence and without fear, by calling Thee, 'Father.' " The Greek text says exactly this:"Thou, ἐπουράνιον Θεὸν (i.e. God on high whom one cannot name, the apophatic God), to name Thee Father and to dare to invoke Thee."[31]

There is no historical evidence that the terms "Father, Son and Holy Spirit" were products of a patriarchal structure, a "male" theology, or a hierarchical church.[32] Rather, all those involved in the Christological and Trinitarian controversies—Athanasios of Alexandria, Basil the Great, Gregory of Nyssa, Gregory the Theologian, and Hilary of Poitiers—had one mission from God: to enable the Church finally to express the Divinity as Unity/Trinity.[33] By their dedication, the Christian God was

[29] Louis Bouyer, *Woman in the Church* (San Francisco, 1979), pp. 29-32.

[30] *Who is the Rich Man who is Saved?* 37, PG 9.641C.

[31] Vladimir Lossky, *Orthodox Theology: An Introduction* (Crestwood, N.Y., 1978), p. 32.

[32] It must be noted particularly that in several historical instances the Church was much fairer toward women than the surrounding culture. Saint Gregory the Theologian, a great Trinitarian theologian, exemplified this by upraiding the men of his flock in regard to a civil law which meted out strict punishment for wives committing adultery, but disregarded punishing husbands committing the same crime: "[Let me discuss] chastity, in respect of which I see that the majority of men are ill-disposed, and that their laws are unequal and irregular. For what was the reason why they restrained the woman, but indulged the man, and that a woman who practices evil against her husband's bed is an adulteress, and the penalties of the law for this are very severe; but if the husband commits fornication against his wife, he has no account to give? I do not accept this legislation; I do not approve this custom. They who made the law were men, and therefore the legislation is hard on women. . . . " *Homily* 37.6 *on Matthew* 19.1-12, PG 36.289A-B.

[33] Lossky, *Orthodox Theology*, p. 38.

explained in accordance with Scripture and in accordance with the Apostolic Faith. The Christian God was not the God of the Neo-Platonists or of Indian religions which dissolved all personal relationships into Nirvana; neither was the Christian God the totally "Unknown God" of the Athenians (Acts 17.22-32). The Christian God was the God who transcended all human categories and was revealed in the personal names, "Father, Son, and Holy Spirit."[34]

These terms are precise theological terms, keys to understanding the Trinity. They are not exchangeable for such feminist formulae as "Mother, Daughter, Holy Spirit," nor even exchangeable for other attributes and activities of God such as "Creator, Savior, and Sanctifier." They have been revealed to humanity to serve as the most adequate language available to describe the three members of the Trinity. Another statement from Gregory of Nyssa fittingly summarizes these thoughts:

> Since then this doctrine is put forth by the Truth itself, it follows that anything which the inventors of pestilent heresies devise besides to subvert this divine utterance—as, for example, calling the Father "Maker" and "Creator" of the Son instead of "Father," and the Son a "result," a "creature," a "product" instead of "Son," and the Holy Spirit the "creature of a creature" and the "product of a product" instead of his proper title the "Spirit," and whatever those who fight against God are pleased to say of him—all such fancies we term a denial and violaton of the Godhead revealed to us in this doctrine. For once for all we have learned from the Lord, through whom comes the transformation of our nature from mortality to immortality—from him, I say, we have learned to what we ought to look with the eyes of our understanding—that is, the Father, the Son, and the Holy Spirit. We say that it is a terrible and soul-destroying thing to misinterpret these divine utterances and to devise in their stead assertions to subvert them—assertions pretending to correct God the Word, who appointed that we should maintain these statements as part of our faith. For each of these titles understood in its natural sense becomes for Christians a rule of truth and a law of piety.[35]

Conclusion

Admittedly, this lecture has been polemical in tone, and narrowly focused in addressing a complex issue. It also has failed to review the

---

[34] Ibid., p. 32.
[35] *Against Eunomios* 2.2, PG 45.468C-469A.

many positive works wrought by the women's movement within Christian denominations, in particular: the historical search for life stories and writings of saintly women; the heightened awareness that women bear charisms which should be exercised for the building up of the Body of Christ; and the expanded presence and impact of women using their gifts in Christian communities.

However, my genuine concern during the lecture has been that the Church be critical of theologies incongruous with what the Spirit of God has revealed throughout the ages of the believing community. The Church must guard against distortions in anthropological or theological thought, so that indeed (remembering the words of Edith Stein): "The things of God can be given back to God;" and (remembering the words of Irenaios of Lyons): "The glory of God may be seen in humanity, and the life of humanity may consist in the vision of God."

Our salvation depends on this. Life in abundance demands it.

Notes on the Contributors

MICHAEL A. FAHEY, S.J. is Professor of Systematic Theology and Director of Graduate Studies, Department of Theological Studies, Concordia University, Montreal, Quebec; an Executive Secretary for the Eastern Orthodox/Roman Catholic Consultation in North America.

DANIEL J. SAHAS is Associate Professor, Department of Religious Studies, University of Waterloo, Waterloo, Ontario; representative of the Greek Orthodox Diocese of Toronto (Ontario) to the General Board of the Canadian Council of Churches.

ROBERT BARRINGER C.S.B. is Assistant Professor, Department of Religious Studies, University of Toronto and Faculty of Theology, Univeristy of St. Michael's College, Toronto; permanent representative of the Archbishop of Toronto for the Orthodox Churches.

DEBORAH BELONICK is a graduate of St. Vladimir's Orthodox Theological Seminary; member Faith and Order Commission, National Council of Churches (U.S.A.); delegate of Orthodox Church in America to W.C.C. conferences in Epiney (1979) and Sheffield (1981); author of *Feminism in Christianity. An Orthodox Christian Response* (Syosset 1983).